MW00677458

ENGLISH
ONLINE

ENGLISH ONLINE

A Student's Guide to the Internet and World Wide Web

Eric Crump
University of Missouri, Columbia

Nick Carbone
Marlboro College

Houghton Mifflin Company   Boston   New York

Sponsoring Editor George Kane
Assistant Editor Jennifer Roderick
Associate Project Editor Elena Di Cesare
Production/Design Coordinator Jennifer Meyer
Electronic Production Supervisor Irene Cinelli
Manufacturing Manager Florence Cadran
Marketing Manager Pamela Laskey

Cover illustration and cover design by Diana Coe.

Printed in the U.S.A.

Library of Congress Catalog Card Number: 96-76886

ISBN: 0-395-76749-0

123456789-SB-00 99 98 97 96

CONTENTS

Preface XV

PART ONE **INTRODUCTION** 1

1 **Introduction to the Online World** 3

1.1 A World Within a World   3
1.2 The Internet   4
1.3 Internet History   4
1.4 Relevance to English Students   5
1.5 Expectations for This Book   7

2 **Netiquette** 8

2.1 Introduction   8
2.2 A Twelve-Step Netiquette Quick Reference   9
2.3 Netiquette for Using the Internet   10

Protect Your Privacy and That of Others   10
Learn and Follow the Acceptable Use Policy   10
Don't Play When Someone Else Needs to Work   11
Always Get Permission for Exceptions to Rules   11

2.4 Netiquette for Communicating on
the Internet   11

Stand by Your Words   11
End E-Mail with Your Name and Address   11
Never Leave the Subject Heading Blank   12
Cross-Post Appropriate Messages Only   12
Practice Frugality   12
Strive for Clarity   12
Give Yourself a Minute to Think About a Message
    Before You Write It   13
Be Tolerant of Errors, Including Your Own   13
Use Accurate Summaries and Judicious Quoting   13
Keep Cool If You've Been Flamed   14

2.5 Netiquette for Acknowledging People and
     Resources on the Internet   14

3 Preparing to Enter the Internet 16

3.1 A Word About Interface   16
3.2 Getting Help with Software   17
3.3 Leave Time for Learning and Error   17

Preview Your Handouts   17
Diagnose Your Mistakes   18

3.4 Dealing with the Enormousness of
     the Internet   19

Create a Mental Picture   19

PART TWO **HOW TO'S 21**

4 Electronic Mail 23

4.1 Introduction   23
4.2 The Speed of E-Mail   24
4.3 E-Mail for Those Who Don't Have
     Anyone to Write To   24
4.4 E-Mail Basics   25
     1. Making Sense of E-Mail Lingo   25

Acronym Shorthand   26
Smileys or Emoticons   26

2. Writing an E-Mail Address   27
3. Using a Subject Line   28

4. Using the Reply Command   29
5. Ending a Message   30
   Signature Files   30
6. Using an Address Book   31
7. Saving Messages into Folders   33
8. Downloading and Uploading Files to Send by E-Mail   33
9. Dealing with Spam Messages   34
10. Dealing with Flames   34

5   Mailing Lists: Hosts for Discussion Groups and Online Communities   36

5.1 Introduction   36
5.2 How Mailing Lists Work   37
   How Much Listspace Is on the Internet?   37
   An Increasing Number of Lists   37
5.3 Mailing List Programs: Listserv, Listproc, and Majordomo   38
5.4 Finding Lists   39
   Listserv Lists   39
   Interest Groups   40
5.5 Subscribing to Lists   40
   Subscribing in Listserv   41
   Subscribing in Listproc   42
   Subscribing in Majordomo   43
5.6 Unsubscribing from Lists   44
   Unsubscribing from Listserv   44
   Unsubscribing from Listproc   44
   Unsubscribing from Majordomo   44
5.7 Mail Options   45
   Listserv Mail Options   45
   Listproc Mail Options   47
   Majordomo Mail Options   48
5.8 Archives   48
   Listserv Archives   48
   Listproc Archives   51

Majordomo Archives   52
Web and Gopher Archives   52

5.9   Common Problems   53
One Wrong Character   54
Right Syntax, Wrong Program   54
Talking to the Wrong People   54
Unintentional Masquerading   55

5.10 Getting Help   55

6 **Telnetting on the Internet 58**
6.1 Introduction   58
6.2 Connecting to a Telnet Database   59

7 **Gopher and Lynx 63**
7.1 Introduction   63
Gopher   64
Lynx   64
Some Brief Words on Navigating   65

7.2 Bookmarking   65
Bookmarking in Gopher   66
Bookmarking in Lynx   67

7.3 Advanced Navigating: Direct Addresses   68
Gopher and Direct Addresses   68
Lynx and Direct Addresses   70

7.4 Saving   71
Saving a File in Gopher   71
Saving a File in Lynx   72

7.5 Downloading Files with Gopher
and Lynx   73
7.6 Searching for Resources in Gopher
and Lynx   74
7.7 Gopher Commands   74
7.8 Lynx Commands   75

8 **File Transfer Protocol 77**
8.1 Introduction   77
8.2 Anonymous FTP   78

9 Getting Freeware and Shareware from
     Public Archives   84

    9.1 Introduction   84
    9.2 Freeware   85
    9.3 Shareware   85
    9.4 Downloading   86
    9.5 Macintosh Decompression Utilities   87
    9.6 Windows Decompression Utilities   88
    9.7 Common Sites for Freeware and Shareware   89

        Macintosh Software Archives   89
        INFO-Mac Mirrors   89
        Windows and DOS Software Archives   90
        Windows and DOS Software Mirrors   90

    9.8 How to FTP Freeware and Shareware for Macs
         and PCs   90

        Failed Connection Messages   92
        Getting Software Files   92
        Variations   94

10 Graphic Browsers   96

    10.1 Introduction   96
    10.2 Netscape   97

        Introduction   97
        Netscape Built-In Features   99
        Other Interface Elements   100
        Where to Find Netscape Navigator Copies and
            Information   102

    10.3 Mosaic   103

        Introduction   103
        Facts About Using Mosaic   104

    10.4 MacWeb and WinWeb   105

        Introduction   105
        MacWeb and WinWeb Particulars   106

    10.5 A Selection of URLs to Explore   107

11 MOOs and MUDs   108

    11.1 Introduction   108

11.2 Telnet Help for MOOing   109
Viewing a MOO in Telnet   110
Sending a Message in Telnet   111
Alternatives to Telnet   112

12 A MOO Walkthrough (Telnet) 115
12.1 Introduction   115
12.2 MOO Etiquette   121

13 OWLs and Other Birds of the Net 123
13.1 OWLs   123
13.2 WIOLEs   125
13.3 List of Sites   126

14 How to Create Your Own Basic Web Page 128
14.1 The Web Changes Everything   128
14.2 Permissions   130
14.3 Introduction to HTML   131
14.4 HTML Basics   132

<H> Headings   133
<P> Paragraphs   133
<L> Lists   133
<A HREF> Links   134
<IMG SRC> Image Source   134

14.5 Sample HTML Document   135
14.6 Basic UNIX Commands   137

PART THREE **RESEARCH** 141

15 Plagiarism, Copyright, and the Internet   143
15.1 Introduction   144
15.2 The Difference Between Paper and Pixels   144
15.3 Three Serious Concerns   145
15.4 Concern One: Honesty   146

Consider the Complexities of Collaboration   147
Keep a Writing Portfolio and Research Log   147
Use Mixed Fonts   148

15.5 Concern Two: Stability and New Forms of
      Scholarship   148

      Brand Names   148
      Institutional Addresses   149
      Personal Addresses   149
      Yes, but What About Stability?   150
      Journals and Peer Review   150
      New Kinds of Academic Excellence   151

15.6 Concern Three: Plagiarism Meets
      Copyright   151

16 Citing Computer Programs and Electronic
        Documents 154

16.1 Tips on Creating Correct Citations   154

      Be Consistent with Other Citations   155
      Don't Be Afraid to Give Too Much Information   155
      Consider Using Explanatory Footnotes When
          Needed   155

16.2 Working with Files Accessed from the
      Internet   155

      Keep Careful Records   155
      Note Version Numbers   156
      Remember That Pagination Will Vary   156
      Indicate Correct Citation Particulars When Using a
          Downloaded File   158

16.3 Citation Guidelines   158

16.4 Modern Language Association (MLA) Style
      Guidelines   159

      Creating a Works-Cited Entry   159
      Working Citations into Your Text   160
      MLA Style for E-Mail   160
      MLA Style for File Transfer Protocol   162
      MLA Style for Gopher   163
      MLA Style for the World Wide Web   164
      MLA Style for MOOs and MUDs and Other Telnet
          Sites   164

16.5 American Psychological Association (APA)
      Style Guidelines   167

      APA Style for E-Mail   169

APA Style for File Transfer Protocol   171
APA Style for Gopher   171
APA Style for the World Wide Web   171

16.6 *The Chicago Manual of Style* (CMS)
Guidelines   172

Computer Information Services and Databases   173
CMS Style for E-Mail   174
CMS Style for File Transfer Protocol   181
CMS Style for Gopher   182
CMS Style for the World Wide Web   183

PART FOUR **RESOURCES 185**

17 E-Mail Lists and USENET Groups:
A Sampler 187

17.1 The Directories   187

The Kovacs Directory   187
Other Recommended Directories   188

17.2 The Lists   188

Literature   188
Writing   189
USENET Groups for Writing and Literature   190
A List for Getting Help   192

18 Learning Online: A List of Resources 193

18.1 Searches   194

Direct (or Keyword) Searches   194
Undirected Searches   195
Subject-Categorized Search Resources   195

18.2 English Departments and Courses   196
18.3 Scholarly Societies   197
18.4 Literature and the Humanities   198
18.5 Writing   199
18.6 A Sampling of Online Writing Labs   199
18.7 General Education Resources   200
18.8 MOO and MUD Resources   200

Help for MOOs and MUDs   201

18.9 Publications   201

Publication Directories 201
Online Journals 202
Online Magazines 203

18.10 Project Gutenberg 204
18.11 Government Resources 205

19 Help with the Internet 206

19.1 Online Books About the Internet 206
19.2 Printed Books About the Internet 207
19.3 Other Online Internet Guides 207
19.4 Help with the World Wide Web 208
19.5 Netiquette and E-Mail Guides 209
19.6 Sites for Internet Tools 209

Web Browsers 209
Other Internet Tools 210

PART FIVE **ACTIVITIES 211**

20 Activities for Students 213

20.1 USENET for Yourself 213
20.2 USENET for English Classes 214
20.3 E-Mail Address Searches 217
20.4 Gopher Searching 219
20.5 Veronica and WAIS 219

Veronica 219
WAIS 220

20.6 Searching the Web 221

Glossary 223

Index 233

PREFACE

With the Internet in a period of exponential growth, information about the Internet is burgeoning as well. Yet this information can be difficult to manage and use. Our goal in writing this book is to help English students and teachers ride the Internet wave to their advantage. A certain amount of frustration is to be expected when encountering an unfamiliar environment, especially a rapidly changing one like the Net. (We've experienced our share indeed.) We hope this guide will help you learn the ways of the Internet more quickly than you would on your own.

This guide is not intended to answer every single question you might have about Internet tools and culture. There are too many local variables that we have no way of anticipating. The Net itself changes so fast that it is impossible to create a perfectly stable source of information and instruction. The best operating instructions for the Net are actually on the Net and are revised continually. We have provided information about how to find many help files and guides, but the best way to learn the technical, social, and educational ways of the Net is to dive right into it.

From that perspective, this book is a starting point on your journey. We will do our best to help you make the transition. After you have read the book we encourage you to visit our web site, where you can post new information, questions, clarifications, and stories about life as English students and teachers. More importantly, the web site allows you to interact with us and in the process help improve the book.

The *English Online* web site is at the following address:
http://www.hmco.com/hmco/college/english/englishonline/
    EnglishOnline.html

And for anyone who does not have access to the web, the authors and editors can be reached via e-mail at College_English@hmco.com.

Organization of *English Online*

This guide is organized by concepts and by specific tools. It is helpful to think of the Internet as both a technical construct—a technological medium made up of communication and information tools and as a social construct—an environment of newly emerging social and educational conventions. We begin our discussion of the Internet by focusing on its social and educational context.

We have used certain conventions in this book to make it easier to use. For example, when we instruct you to type something, it will appear like this:

    Type **this**

Internet examples appear in a special typeface to represent what you will see on-screen, like this:

    This is an example of on-screen text.

Introduction

This section provides a foundation for using the tools described in subsequent sections. It offers guidance on the evolving culture of the Net, its relevance to English students, and the acceptable norms of behavior known as "netiquette."

How To's

This section contains chapters that take you through the basic steps for using the most common tools on the Net, including:

- **Electronic Mail**   perhaps the most common method of communicating on the Internet
- **Mailing Lists**   allow groups of people to discuss matters of common interest
- **Telnet**   allows people to use resources at other sites on the Net almost as if they were at each site
- **File Transfer Protocol (FTP)**   sends and receives files from one computer to another

- **Gopher** finds and receives information, based on an easy-to-use hierarchical system of organization
- **World Wide Web Browsers (Lynx, Netscape, Mosaic, and MacWeb)** use a hypertextual system of finding, receiving, and publishing information on the Net
- **Multiple-User Environments (MOOs)** provide real-time communication and offer possibilities for creating and extending the virtual environment

We've tried at every possible opportunity to make our explanations and examples relevant to the interests of English students. The examples lead you to resources we hope will prove both interesting and useful in your studies. And they not only teach you how to use a particular tool, but they also introduce you to the online English community.

Research

This section covers the subjects of plagiarism, copyright, and citation of sources. These things are difficult enough to understand in the stable world of print—imagine how complex they become in the changeable world of the Net! New capabilities introduced by new technologies confuse the issues surrounding research. This section of the book attempts to shed some light on the complexity of online research and help you to adapt new tools to an old function. We offer practical advice and guidance on how to avoid plagiarism, respect copyright, and properly cite sources.

Resources

The Resources section expands on what is covered in the How To's section. It provides instruction on how to use the new tools you have learned and cites online sources for additional information.

Activities

A common question teachers and students have when first introduced to the Internet is, "This stuff is all very interesting and fun, but how can I use it in my class?" The Activities section of this book tries to answer that question by suggesting activities that fit well with many English courses and introduce students to valuable Internet resources. We hope the *English Online* web site will be a forum where we can all continue compiling assignments and activities, extending this section of the book indefinitely.

Glossary

The Internet has its own special vocabulary that can be difficult to understand. The Glossary section of this book is a good introduction to many of the terms specific to the computing and network worlds. This is another section that may lend itself to collaborative extension via the book's web site.

Acknowledgments

We would like to express our deep appreciation to the many people who contributed to the development of this book. First, of course, a nod and a hug to our families—Amy, Flannery, and Quincy Crump, and Barbara Crowley-Carbone and Nicole and Emma Carbone—who graciously tolerated our obsession with the Net and our preoccupation with the book. We owe immeasurable debt to our colleagues on the Net, a bright and supportive group of teachers, students, and scholars. Everything we know about the Net is a direct result of working in such a rich learning environment with such terrific people. There are too many people to name. We are grateful to the wonderful and very patient people at Houghton Mifflin, especially George Kane and Jennifer Roderick, who helped us initiate this project and who strongly influenced its shape. Elena Di Cesare, Jennifer Meyer, and Irene Cinelli worked on the production of the book, and Victoria Keirnan helped set up the web site. Many people provided us with useful reviews: Kris Bair, Fort Hays State University (KS); Geoffrey Chase, Northern Arizona State University; Yuet-Sim D. Chiang, University of California, Berkeley; Alexander Friedlander, Drexel University (PA); Karen R. Hamer, Pittsburgh State University (KS); Roger Johnson, Lewis-Clark State College (ID); Deborah Balzhiser Morton, University of Minnesota; John Peterson, University of California, Irvine; Peter R. Vanderhoof, Peninsula College (WA); and Janice R. Walker, University of South Florida. Special thanks to A. Dean Fontenot, Texas Tech University, who ensured the book's technical accuracy. And finally, we would like to thank you. We hope that readers of this book will use it to find their way online, resulting in productive new connections and collaborations.

Eric Crump
Nick Carbone

Eavesdropping on the Authors

What follows is a conversation between the authors that took place on a MOO. It seemed appropriate to use one of the tools described in the book to create part of the preface. For more information about MOOs, see Chapters 11 and 12.

Nick says, "So what do you think of our preface? Did we cover all the major points, such as why we wrote the book?"

Eric says, "We wanted to do this because we felt too many people were worried about getting started online. This book helps people take their first plunge into the Net."

Nick says, "Exactly. It's not comprehensive. If it were, then it would keep growing and be re-released every other day :). But it does offer a place to begin."

Eric says, "Right. It's like a pocket version of the American Heritage Dictionary: light, portable, and easy to use."

Nick says, "We did make some choices in our approach that differ from other Internet guides. For instance, we include examples for lower-tech connections, whereas other guides assume only high-tech ones."

Eric says, "The web site is an extension of what's covered in the book. I think of the book as an inviting hallway and the web site as the rooms leading off it."

Nick says, "And maybe if people like a particular room they'll decide to stay a while, even MOOve in ;)."

PART one

INTRODUCTION

Chapter 1. Introduction to the Online World
Chapter 2. Netiquette
Chapter 3. Preparing to Enter the Internet

CHAPTER 1

Introduction to the Online World

CHAPTER CONTENTS
1.1   A World Within a World
1.2   The Internet
1.3   Internet History
1.4   Relevance to English Students
1.5   Expectations for This Book

1.1   A World Within a World

It is bigger than any nation. It is as small as a cozy booth in a neighborhood café. By some accounts, its population is growing faster than the world's. By other accounts, its population estimates are grossly inflated. Depending on your perspective, it can either bring about social revolution or support the status quo. It contains vast quantities of information though finding the right information at the right time is not yet a simple matter for most users. It fosters intelligent discussion of issues, mindless prattle, and the sinister dealings of society's lunatic fringe. It liberates and enslaves. It is home to paradox and disorientation, to joy and excitement, to hyperbolic rhetoric and misinformation. It is the online world, the social environment that resides in the global network of people using computers to communicate. Right now the most dynamic part of the online world is the Internet.

Trying to capture the Internet in words reminds us of the parable of the blind men trying to describe an elephant. The one who grabbed the tail was sure the beast resembled a rope. The one who wrapped his arms around a thick leg was sure that it was very similar to a tree. The one who latched onto the trunk concluded that the animal was related to the snake. Likewise, the Internet, or Net for short, is a different critter depending on which piece of it you happen to grab.

1.2 The Internet

The Internet is a vast system of interconnected computer networks. These networks—distinct online worlds in themselves—connected to the Internet vary widely in size (geographic area and population), bandwidth (information volume), technological sophistication, and purpose. What holds them together is not a central authority but a central principle: cooperation—both technical and social. Administrators of each network agree to use certain technical protocols that allow diverse and otherwise incompatible machinery to interact, opening electronic conduits for almost any kind of information imaginable. The result is a networked system that no one owns but to which everyone contributes.

Like its machinery, the culture of the Net is based on collaboration, cooperation, and sharing. If that sounds unrealistically idyllic, it is and it isn't. Along with nice collegial sharing and friendship, people are quick to share their anger, their cynicism, and their paranoia. People in this culture tend to share more. But just what they share, or whether sharing is always a good thing, are open questions.

1.3 Internet History

Any extensive history of the Internet might start as far back as the introduction of the telegraph, the first use of electricity to communicate over distance. For our purposes, though, the history of the Internet begins in the early 1960s, in the heart of the cold war. The U.S. government became interested in developing a communication system that would survive a nuclear attack. The Defense Department's Advanced Research Projects Agency (ARPA) was called upon to create the system. Researchers realized that the system would have to be decentralized so that no one part was essential to the operation of the whole. The beginnings of the Internet began to take shape in the early 1970s when researchers and technologists at a handful of universities developed the protocol (which became TCP/IP, Transmission Control Protocol/Internet Protocol) that would allow different computer systems to communicate with one another. Until the late 1980s, the system was primarily used by university and government scientists and technologists.

However, as tools for communicating and sharing information became easier to use, the popularity of the Internet grew throughout society: in universities, businesses, libraries, and other organizations. And like the personal computer movement of the late 1970s, the use of the Internet is now beginning to spread to the home. Businesses are the fastest growing users of the Net, and individuals are quickly following, ready (more or less) to begin shopping there for goods and entertainment. Just as the telegraph led to the telephone, which quickly reshaped our entire society, the Internet appears poised to do the same, with perhaps even more profound implications.

1.4 Relevance to English Students

English studies are concerned with language and literacy, with the conventions and possibilities of creating art and communicating ideas with words. Although we have not traditionally recognized it, literacy and technology are inextricably intertwined. Print technology has dominated language arts for the past few centuries, and our conceptions of literacy have been shaped by the features of that technology. The emergence of computer networks as venues for communication and community will affect the fundamental shapes of literacy. Writers and readers now must understand how communication and literary arts work in electronic environments that both resemble and differ from print.

Electronic writing in some ways fundamentally differs from its print predecessor. Differences in speed and scale require that readers and writers in network environments acquire new skills and new sensibilities while maintaining contact with the ever-important world of print. Writing and reading tend to happen faster in network environments. As a result, writing tends to be more conversational and informal. People also generally write for smaller groups as opposed to the large audience of a print publication.

Print calls for precision and efficiency because writers are limited by the number of words or pages available in publications. Therefore, print generally involves refinement, revising the text in an effort to express the ideas in a concise and logical way. In online (i.e., computerized) venues, writing comes to mean something different. It is more conversational because readers can respond immediately. Ideas develop as part of those interactions with others. Clarity evolves through continued interaction—accumulation rather than purification. And space for all those words, though not infinite, is cheap and vast.

At the same time, the sensibilities of print culture exert a strong influence on people as they move to electronic or Internet writing environments. In many cases, teachers and students find ways to make these new electronic writing tools perform the same functions old writing tools did. Students may be asked to converse via e-mail, for example, but their conversations will be part of an essay that is judged by print conventions. The status quo dies hard.

The Internet is very relevant to English students. We will provide instruction on how to use the most common Internet tools for finding information and bringing new information online, as well as for communicating with others. We will suggest ways to put those tools to good use and will point to locations and projects on the Internet that are designed for English scholars and writers, such as online journals, electronic versions of books, student-run multimedia publications, sites for publishing student work, and courses taught online. We also offer comments on the history and culture of the Net as we know it—the social environment in which these tools were developed and continue to evolve.

1.5 Expectations for This Book

Writing an introductory guide to the Internet is in some ways a task destined to fail—at least it will fail to satisfy readers who expect definitive descriptions that will apply year after year. We are working with a moving target, a world that is in the volatile and transformative early stage of life (and that's what we like about it). Be suspicious of anyone who claims to know the Truth of the online world, who presumes to reveal all its secrets. We claim only to describe as best we can the parts we know well—as they exist now while we write this book.

As for the tail and the trunk and all the parts between, well, discovery is part of the fun. The Internet is vast, and although people disagree on how vast, there is much to explore. Because this particular animal keeps changing, we will learn more about it as the book finds its way into print. We hope this book will be a good start for your exploration, and we invite you to share your experiences. In conjunction with Houghton Mifflin, we have set up a homepage on the World Wide Web for updates and for collecting reader feedback. You and other readers will learn things about the Internet and its resources for English majors that we do not yet know. The address for the homepage is **http://www.hmco.com/**. This takes you to the Houghton Mifflin Company Homepage; from there, you will find a link to the page for *English Online*. You can also reach us by e-mail at **College_English@hmco.com**. And don't worry, if you skip to the chapters in this manual on the World Wide Web and e-mail, you will learn all you need to know about how to use these addresses.

CHAPTER 2

Netiquette

CHAPTER CONTENTS
2.1 Introduction
2.2 A Twelve-Step Netiquette Quick Reference
2.3 Netiquette for Using the Internet
2.4 Netiquette for Communicating on the Internet
2.5 Netiquette for Acknowledging People and Resources on the Internet

2.1 Introduction

The word netiquette combines "net," short for "Internet," and "etiquette." Etiquette on the Internet, like etiquette everywhere else, works best when seasoned with a little tolerance, compassion, and humor. Good netiquette requires observing the customs of the Net, much as knowing the customs and habits of where you travel makes you more welcome. The Internet is foremost about bringing people together. As much as it is praised for the

2.2 A Twelve-Step Netiquette Quick Reference

Access Rules
1. Always learn and follow the acceptable use policy (AUP).
2. Don't tie up computers in public labs with game playing when other people need to work and are waiting for a terminal.

E-mail Rules
3. Always end your messages with your name and e-mail address.
4. Always include a subject heading with e-mail.
5. Only forward a message if it is appropriate and if doing so will not harm the reputation of the writer. If in doubt, get permission to forward the message from the original sender.
6. In e-mail, always use judicious quoting.
7. Take reasonable care with your punctuation and spelling, and don't write in all capitals SINCE IT LOOKS AS IF YOU ARE SHOUTING.

Research and Citation Rules
8. If you quote e-mail in another venue—a paper, an article, an online essay—try to get permission from the writer you are quoting.
9. Always give proper credit for anything you use or find on the Internet.
10. Make sure you write down all the information needed for others to go to the source you have cited.

Honesty and Decorum Rules
11. Never use shareware (software available to the public at low prices and paid for on the honor system) without paying the fee for it.
12. If you get flamed, do not flame in return. Stay cool and respond with wit and good humor. It will make you look cool and make the flamer look bad.

vast amounts of information available to users, that information is secondary to the people with whom you can communicate.

There are three general categories of netiquette: netiquette for using the Internet, netiquette for communicating on the Internet, and netiquette for acknowledging people and resources on the Internet. Like any set of rules or advice, following them requires good judgment. Much of the advice we outline here will also be covered in other sections of the book. For example, when we discuss e-mail in Chapter 4, you will read more about e-mail netiquette. Our purpose here is to give you in one section a compendium of the types of netiquette that help make the Internet a useful resource.

2.3 Netiquette for Using the Internet

Protect Your Privacy and That of Others

First, remember that your e-mail is not secure. It can be read by system administrators or anyone who may have your password. This will not usually be a problem, but it is always a good idea to put any e-mail you consider sensitive onto your own computer or a floppy disk. To help protect your privacy, choose a password to your account that is a combination of numbers and characters that do not spell a word or common phrase. For example, TEA4TWO would be fairly easy to hack, whereas T&8GM44 would be much harder.

Learn and Follow the Acceptable Use Policy

Netiquette on use is usually described in acceptable use policies and rules set forth by the company or service that provides your Internet access. For most of you reading this book, it will be policies set by your school. These may include limits on the amount of information you can store on your account, in either file number or total amount of bytes, or limits on when you can use the Internet recreationally, as with MUDs (Multi-User Dimensions) or IRC (Internet Relay Chat), two tools associated with chatting and playing games such as Dungeons and Dragons.

Don't Play When Someone Else Needs to Work

Although we can think of no academic computer network whose sole purpose is to be a virtual arcade, we haven't yet heard of one where there isn't some online game. Playing games is fine, as long as it's in moderation and does not interfere with the work of others.

Always Get Permission for Exceptions to Rules

Many teachers use software associated with games, like MUDs or MOOs (Multi-User Dimensions—Object Oriented), as places for classes to meet online. Students also use these tools for research and to meet other scholars who are interested in the same academic subjects. The resource chapter in this manual lists educational MOOs you can visit. If your purpose in using tools normally associated with gaming is educational, that's wonderful. However, you should still follow your school's acceptable use policy unless you get permission to do otherwise. Many administrators will allow an exception if they understand how you are using the tools.

2.4 Netiquette for Communicating on the Internet

Stand by Your Words

You should always be accountable for what you write and say. Don't write or send anything on the Internet, or anywhere else for that matter, that you are not ready to stand by. This does not mean you cannot change your mind or eventually come around to another point of view. It means you should think about what you want to say, and say it as clearly as you can. On the Internet, you exist primarily in the words you write. What you say *is* who you are in an online world; it is the only way most people online will ever know you.

End E-Mail with Your Name and Address

People usually overlook this point of netiquette because they assume another user will be able to see or know their e-mail and name automatically. This is not always the case. Thus your name and address become important, especially when sending mail to a discussion list or to USENET (an Internet-wide collection of discussion groups). Your address makes it easier for others to respond directly to you, but only if you include it at the end of your message.

Never Leave the Subject Heading Blank

Many people have software that automatically deletes messages without a subject heading. Others use their own personal filter— the delete key. Blank subject headings reduce your chances of being read; they cripple communication. The only time you will want a blank subject heading is when sending messages to some discussion list software, such as LISTSERV.

Cross-Post Appropriate Messages Only

Some messages you read might encourage you to forward them, for example, announcements of literary contests, internships, or job openings. Others might happen to coincide with a discussion you are having on another list or in another forum, say, a classroom. You should cross-post these latter types only if you are certain the writer would not mind; the best way to be certain is to get permission.

Practice Frugality

We use the word *frugal* here, instead of the usual term *brevity,* to stress that we do not mean all messages must be short, but instead that all messages should try to use words as thoughtfully as possible for two reasons: people often have a lot of e-mail to sort through and may not bother to finish rambling messages, and being frugal increases your chances of being understood. Be frugal with your ideas; don't waste words by treating them cheaply.

Strive for Clarity

Clarity can suffer for any number of reasons. It is sometimes lost because the writer and reader do not share the same context or frame of reference. For example, on one list, a writer sent a message recommending an article in CCC. Many people on the list did not know CCC referred to a journal called *College Composition and Communication*. Sometimes clarity is lost for technical reasons: a bad connection results in a message with strange, unintelligible characters. At other times, a message will be unclear because of a typo or punctuation error. As you can see, some confusion is inevitable. However, there are steps you can take to keep it to a minimum.

Give Yourself a Minute to Think About a Message Before You Write It

Most electronic messages are written quickly; it is one of the charms of the medium. This is especially true for real-time (or simultaneous) discussions, such as MOOs and MUDs, where two or more users agree to log on to the Internet at the same time. People know that there will be more typos and misspellings because participants are literally writing as they think, and what they write is being read almost the instant it is keyed in.

However, in writing such as e-mail, USENET, and World Wide Web discussion forums, messages are sent for others to read and respond to later. Since there is more of a time lag, people generally expect fewer errors than they do in real-time forums. When writing e-mail, try to take a moment to write the message first in your head. A quick planning session will help you be both frugal and clear.

Be Tolerant of Errors, Including Your Own

Taking care to avoid errors is best. However, you do not want to write e-mail as if you were taking a test. You will write both good messages and embarrassing ones, so treat errors kindly. Never publicly correct someone for an error in spelling or punctuation, especially since many e-mail programs lack spell-checking software. If an error distorts the meaning of a message beyond your understanding, e-mail the writer privately and ask for clarification.

Use Accurate Summaries and Judicious Quoting

The Reply command on most e-mail and USENET (the global discussion list service) Reader programs offer you a choice of including the original message in your reply. If you say yes, delete any portion of the original message that is not relevant. For example, if you are responding to only two sentences in a forty-sentence message, delete all but those two sentences. You can summarize the other thirty-eight sentences in a line or two if needed.

Keep Cool If You've Been Flamed

A flame is a message that is full of invective, spit, and fury. Flames vary in heat and intensity, and some are actually unintentional. Flaming can change the atmosphere of an Internet community the way a mugging changes the atmosphere of a street. On some groups, flaming is to be expected. Anywhere politics or social policy is discussed, there are likely to be flames. The worst flames attack a person's character instead of his or her argument. Some USENET groups are famous for their flame wars, pitched battles of e-mail invectives. According to Chuq Von Rospach's *A Primer on How to Work with the USENET Community,* one of the most common sources of flame wars is when people try to correct someone's grammar or punctuation.

Many times people feel they've been flamed when in fact no flame was intended. Take a moment to consider what was written, and respond to it thoughtfully and patiently. If you are unsure of what the author intended, ask. If you have been flamed, it is better to respond with wit and humor. Keeping cool is always a good idea. Even if you get a particularly virulent flame, defend yourself with tact. Be sure to criticize the argument and not the person.

2.5 Netiquette for Acknowledging People and Resources on the Internet

The final area of netiquette has to do with attribution. Correct attribution of sources has always been important in English studies and scholarship, as it is with any academic discipline. This is perhaps even more true for the Internet. Many sites offer online resources that can be downloaded and used as handouts. For example, Purdue University has an Online Writing Lab (OWL) that offers guides to grammar and punctuation. Students and teachers are welcome to download these, but are asked to keep the headings on so that others know the handouts originated at

Purdue's OWL. Whenever you borrow from or refer to online sources, be sure to acknowledge them. If you are unsure of the attribution policy of a site, check with your instructor or e-mail the site administrator.

CHAPTER

Preparing to Enter
the Internet

CHAPTER CONTENTS
3.1 A Word About Interface
3.2 Getting Help with Software
3.3 Leave Time for Learning and Error
3.4 Dealing with the Enormousness of the Internet

3.1 A Word About Interface

In this chapter of *English Online* we cover how to use different tools available to you on the Internet. The dilemma we face is having no way to anticipate all the varied types of access, computer software, and experience our readers will have. The term *interface* refers to the combination of all three of these. You might, for example, log onto the Internet by modem via an account with a bulletin board service from an IBM-style computer, perhaps using Microsoft Windows, or perhaps from a program that runs on DOS. Or you might be using a Macintosh with an Ethernet connection to your campus network from which you have immediate access to the Internet. Your e-mail program might be easy to use—with many of the same kinds of point-and-click features you are familiar with in other computer applications—and you may feel comfortable navigating the screen it presents, using the commands, and sending mail. Or you might have a program that requires you to remember a number of commands that you will have to type. The different types of interface combinations, though not quite endless, are daunting.

3.2   Getting Help with Software

To begin using the Internet, you need to make sure you have the documentation that is available for the software you are using. If you are accessing the Net from an educational provider, you may have received some handouts and guides from campus computing support services. On most campuses, the department that sets up computers and manages user accounts will also provide help to users. If you have not already done this, you should write down the phone number and e-mail address of the user support services on your campus. Write the numbers in the front and back of this book; if you own your computer, tape the numbers near your screen. The first question to ask when you call is how to get any of the documentation they have for users. Most support services will offer help sheets and other forms of documentation that are much more helpful than the documentation provided by the software manufacturer.

3.3   Leave Time for Learning and Error

Preview Your Handouts

Once you have the handouts and other materials from your campus help center, you should read the directions *several times* before you begin an actual procedure. Bear in mind that reading the directions can be alienating at first since they often contain lots of computer jargon. Further, sometimes the directions make sense only as you are actually doing a procedure. Take your time and do the best you can; try not to be intimidated by excessive jargon or the need to use commands and procedures that seem as mysterious as a shaman's incantations. Follow the steps and see what happens.

Be patient as you work through the help sheets. Even when they are perfectly understandable, many things can cause an error, for example, mistyping a command, accidentally hitting the wrong command key (such as the Ctrl key instead of the Alt key), or clicking the wrong icon. One of the most common mistakes with new users is that they forget their own passwords or remember them incorrectly.

Diagnose Your Mistakes

Mistakes fall into two general categories. The first is where you make the wrong choice, but the software thinks it is a valid choice. For example, you accidentally change an entry in your e-mail address book. As far as the computer is concerned, no error has been made, so for these kinds of mistakes, it's up to you to notice that something has gone wrong.

The second type of error occurs when you type in unacceptable data, and the software refuses to go on. For example, you enter the wrong password. Sometimes the software will repeat the step at which you made an error or flash an error message, in which case you would have a second chance to enter the data correctly. For example, if you make an error at the login prompt, the prompt will usually return, and you can try again. After a set number of tries without success, however, the program will usually disconnect you from that step, sending you back to the previous step.

Very often the latter type of error occurs with UNIX, a case-sensitive computer operating system common on the Internet. Case sensitive means you must type the command with *exact* capitalization. If the command to start your e-mail program is **pine**, but you type **Pine**, you will get an error message saying, "Command not found." UNIX will not recognize the command with the capital P. Unfortunately the error message will not say, "Sorry, but you need to retype the command with a lowercase p." You have to figure out your own mistake.

As you can see, computer software requires some small degree of precision from users. Software has only as much logic as a programmer gives it, and no programmer can anticipate every type of human error. You must learn the software's logic, or at least enough of it to make the software work.

HELPFUL HINT: Always assume a system will be case sensitive, especially when using Gopher (a menulike program used for moving among computers connected to the Internet), e-mail, USENET, and the World Wide Web. If you type in an address in Gopher or on the Web, type it exactly as it is given to you. In e-mail and USENET do the same.

When you are having trouble with software on the Internet, go slowly and write down what happens as well as any messages the software gives you. This way, when you ask for help, you'll be able to tell user support services exactly what happened. Remember, it's best to try out new software when you can take your time. If you're under pressure, you'll be less likely to write things down and more likely to make a mistake.

3.4 Dealing with the Enormousness of the Internet

The Internet is so big, offers so many different ways of being accessed and traversed, that dealing with all the choices and excitement about the Internet is a task in itself. You need to find a way to resist the pull into information overload and the seduction of thinking you need to know everything and try everything at once. There are learning curves to all that you will discover in this book. The slope of those curves and the time it takes you to ascend them depends on your computer experience and your ability to conceptualize what you are doing.

Create a Mental Picture

Much of the software you use will provide you with familiar metaphors—often in the form of icons—to help guide you. You probably already know some software metaphors: the screen is a desktop; your work is saved in a file and put in a folder; your e-mail has an in-box. To feel comfortable on the Internet, you need a mental picture that works for you, some image to help orient and ground yourself in a world that has no ground, only space—cyberspace.

We believe that as you learn more about cyberspace and explore the online world, one of the best things you can do is create a visual image or metaphor for yourself of what the experience is like. When you do, we'd like to hear what it is. On the web page for *English Online* we'll collect and share with you and others the best metaphors and images our readers create. You are English students; we invite you also to be writers, to be poets.

To get you started, let us tell you one of our favorites. To us, the Internet is not an information superhighway, it's a city. It has twisting alleys and busy thoroughfares. Its neighborhoods include academic communities, business districts, recreational areas, and local salons. It is a city populated by people from all over the world. It is a city whose streets, neighborhoods, and buildings are laid out on the geography of ideas rather than land.

PART

two

HOW TO'S

Chapter 4. Electronic Mail

Chapter 5. Mailing Lists: Hosts for Discussion
Groups and Online Communities

Chapter 6. Telnetting on the Internet

Chapter 7. Gopher and Lynx

Chapter 8. File Transfer and Protocol

Chapter 9. Getting Freeware and Shareware
from Public Archives

Chapter 10. Graphic Browsers

Chapter 11. MOOs and MUDs

Chapter 12. A MOO Walkthrough (Telnet)

Chapter 13. OWLs and Other Birds of the
Net

Chapter 14. How to Create Your Own Basic
Web Page

*The language is not flattering; it's flourishing. At this point in
history, most of the evolution of language, most of the richness
in language, is happening in the [online] space that we are
creating.*
—Kevin Kelly, Harper's, *August 1995*

CHAPTER 4

Electronic Mail

CHAPTER CONTENTS
4.1 Introduction
4.2 The Speed of E-Mail
4.3 E-Mail for Those Who Don't Have Anyone
to Write To
4.4 E-Mail Basics

4.1 Introduction

Electronic mail, or e-mail, remains the most popular way to use
the Internet. We certainly recommend it as the best place to
begin. With e-mail as a starting point, you can learn a lot about
English literature and writing, and, at the same time, learn about
a very practical and necessary application. Yes, necessary.
Familiarity with e-mail will be an expected skill in many of the
employment markets English graduates will enter, including the
academic market. Knowing how to use e-mail will become as necessary as knowing how to use the telephone. If you stop to think
of all the ways the telephone shapes your life—making appoint-

ments, checking in with friends, ordering take-out food, getting a date, conducting business—you'll get an idea of how important e-mail will become as a means of communication. We are so accustomed to telephones, we hardly think about them any more. In time, e-mail will become just as commonplace. But until that time, it helps to have an overview of e-mail as you prepare to use it.

4.2 The Speed of E-Mail

E-mail is not quite the same as postal mail, or what regular e-mail users call "snail mail" because of its slower delivery time. Half the fun of sending postal mail has always been the anticipation of a response. E-mail's speed accentuates anticipation and makes it exciting. There's nothing quite like sending a note to someone on the other side of the country (or the world for that matter) and having him or her write back that same day. What might take a week or so by snail mail could take no more than an hour by e-mail. It could conceivably occur faster—almost instantly—if the person happens to be reading his or her e-mail when you send the message. However, the rapid response time can create new kinds of pressures. Waiting a week to reply to snail mail is not at all unusual, but in e-mail it is a long time. So as you enter the world of e-mail and e-mail discussion lists, keep in mind the time factor and the expectation that response should come sooner rather than later.

Many students use e-mail because they have friends at other colleges who have it, and it's cheaper than a phone call. Others use it because they can contact professors or other students from their classes. Still others may be curious about it but don't have anyone they can write to just yet. So how do you begin using it if you don't know anyone to write to?

4.3 E-Mail for Those Who Don't Have Anyone to Write To

As English students, you are concerned with reading literature and writing, two activities that become much more enjoyable and productive if you can talk to others about what you are reading and writing. One way to begin using e-mail, then, even if you don't personally know anyone else who uses it, is to join discussion groups that center on topics you are reading and writing about as an English student. For example, if you are taking a course in the nineteenth-century British novel, you can support your reading and class discussion of *Pride and Prejudice* by joining the e-mail discussion list Austen-L. The discussion list for Anglo Saxon and Medieval literature, Ansax-L, offers a rich and multitextured consideration by participants who come to the list with a passion for the literature. As you know from having teachers who were passionate about the subjects they taught or from discussions with friends on topics you cared deeply about, there is no better discussion to be had than that with people who are involved in it by choice and love of the topic. E-mail discussion lists are one of the best ways to meet these kinds of people.

4.4 E-Mail Basics

To work comfortably with an e-mail program, you should know how to:

1. Make sense of e-mail lingo
2. Write an e-mail address
3. Use a subject line
4. Use the reply command
5. End a message
6. Use an address book
7. Save messages into folders
8. Download and upload files to send by e-mail
9. Deal with spam messages
10. Deal with flames

You can do more, but if you can manage these steps, in this approximate order, you will be well on your way to happy and productive e-mailing.

1. Making Sense of E-Mail Lingo

We've already mentioned the term *snail mail*, which refers to physical mail moved over land. Many e-mail terms refer to e-mail's speed. Others are born of a writer's need to make sure he or she is not being taken the wrong way. In the pursuit of the sometimes mutually exclusive goals of writing quickly and not being misunderstood, e-mail use has developed two phenomena: the acronym and the emoticon.

Acronym Shorthand

Writers use acronyms as a shorthand in messages to save time and space although not much is really saved per message. We think people use acronyms for their catchiness. Acronyms indicate the writer is "in" on e-mail lingo. Here is a brief list. Often, if you ask someone what one of these means, you will be teased for being a "newbie," a new user on the Internet. Thus the desire to be "in."

BTW	by the way
FWIW	for what it's worth
FYI	for your information
IMO	in my opinion
IMHO	in my humble/honest opinion
TIA	thanks in advance
RTFM	read the f***ing manual
LOL	laughed or laughing out loud
ROTFL	rolling on the floor laughing
YMMV	your mileage may vary (This comes from the little disclaimer tacked onto auto advertisements. It usually means, "What I say may not apply for you.")

Smileys or Emoticons

These are little drawings made with a sequence of typewriter keys. Writers place them at key points in their writing to help signal their intent. People especially rely on them when they want to be sure a point they are making will get across in the intended tone. Sometimes they are used for emphasis as well. Here are some of the most common ones.

:-)	A basic smiley. Some use it to indicate light sarcasm or humor. Occasionally it is used to soften criticism. We've seen it used to express joy.
;-)	A winking smiley. Often used to mean "just kidding."
:-(	A sad face. Sometimes used to show sympathy; some-

times used to reflect how the writer feels about a topic or issue.

:-0   An expression of surprise or shock.

:-| An expression of grim determination or indifference depending on the context.

:->   An expression of sarcasm or archness.

>;->   A winking, arch devil. Chances are a lewd remark was made.

In the netiquette overview in Chapter 2, we talked about being careful with your words. Many guides will advise you to use smileys when attempting sarcasm or irony because doing so will help eliminate or reduce misunderstandings. This may or may not be the case. How and when you use smileys depends on how much fun you are having with your writing and who your audience is.

E-mail does have its complications. The high volume of e-mail forces quick reading and frequent deleting of messages. People often gripe about overflowing in-boxes containing many messages that are a waste of time, although the truth is they would not be overwhelmed if they weren't on so many lists. As you work in e-mail, keep in mind that from time to time you will be annoyed by these messages. The best thing to do is :) and GOWI (get on with it—an acronym we just made up).

2. Writing an E-Mail Address

E-mail addresses are made up of two parts separated by an @ sign. The first part is the username; often it's the login name of the user. This always comes to the left of the @. To the right of the @ is the domain name. Take, for example, the e-mail address for Nick:

Domain names are used as part of the Internet's Domain Name System (DNS), a method of naming host computers that access the Internet. This helps make remembering Internet addresses easier. One thing to note when sending e-mail is the different endings domain names can take. Here are some domain name endings and the sites they indicate:

edu   for *edu*cational site
gov   for *gov*ernment site
mil   for *mil*itary site
com   for a business or person accessing from a *com*mercial
          site
ca   for *Ca*nada
net   often for an Inter*net* service provider
uk   for the *U*nited *K*ingdom

It sometimes helps to compare an e-mail address to a postal address. Using Nick as an example, we notice that a postal address has a consistent hierarchy:

Postal Address	Elements
Nick Carbone	Name
c/o English Department	Academic Department
UMass, Amherst	Institution
Amherst, MA 01002	City, State, and Zip Code

The same hierarchy applies to an e-mail address:

E-Mail Address	Elements
nickc	Login Name
@	Separator
english	Academic Department
umass	Institution
edu	Educational Site

3. Using a Subject Line

Subject lines are very important in e-mail because they tell what the message is about. A good subject line helps the reader make sense of the purpose of the e-mail. Accurate subject lines are very important in distribution lists and bulletin boards that have many users. The subject line identifies which conversational "thread" the message is part of, allowing users who aren't participating in that strand to delete those messages. If you change the topic of discussion, you should also change the subject line. If the new topic arises from an old discussion, it is best to indicate as much so that readers following the older discussion are aware of the change. So a first message might say "Bleak House" in the subject line. Subsequent discussion on it might have messages with "Re: Bleak House" in the subject line. If someone wanted to change the thread of discussion, called "thread" in netspeak, he or she might use "Dickens and Lawyers, was Bleak House."

Because subject lines are so important in e-mail, almost every e-mail program will offer you a prompt that asks you to fill in the subject line. Some, such as the Elm e-mail program, will even ask if you want to cancel a message if you neglect to put in a subject line.

4. Using the Reply Command

Every e-mail program we have ever heard of has a Reply command. It allows a user to press a letter (usually r) or some other key to automatically address an e-mail message to the sender, whether he or she is on an e-mail discussion list or a personal correspondent. Using the Reply command is so easy that many users do it automatically, without thinking about when they should use it. Knowing when to use the Reply command essentially means knowing how to read the headers—information that comes at the top of a message—on your e-mail. Headers will tell you where a message will go if you use the Reply command. Consider the following header as it appears in the Elm e-mail program:

Date: Sun, 18 Jun. 1995 14:01:51 -0500 (CDT)
Subject: e-essays on your call for submission (fwd)
X-Sender: wleric@gold.missouri.edu
To: Nick Carbone <nickc@english.umass.edu>

This header comes from a message from Eric to Nick on June 18. It's direct e-mail and replying will automatically send a message to Eric. The next header is from a message Eric sent to RHETNT-l, a discussion list for rhetoric and writing.

Date: Sat, 17 Jun 1995 20:24:24 -0500
From: Eric Crump <wleric@SHOWME.MISSOURI.EDU>
Subject: Book Explores a Subversive Future for Scholarly Journals (fwd)

Sender: CyberJournal for Rhetoric and Writing <RHETNT-L@MIZ-ZOU1.MISSOURI.EDU>
X-Sender: wleric@showme.missouri.edu (Unverified)
To: Multiple recipients of list RHETNT-L <RHETNT-L@MIZZOU1.MIS-SOURI.EDU>
Reply-to: CyberJournal for Rhetoric and Writing <RHETNT-L@MIZ-ZOU1.MISSOURI.EDU>

The key to using the Reply command is knowing where it will send your reply. Most of the mail sent directly to you will not have a Reply-to line (see the first example). For mail that comes to you via a list, you will usually see a Reply-to option. Sending a message to a list when you think it is going to only one person can be embarrassing. If you were on RHETNT-L and wanted to reply directly to Eric, perhaps with something only he and you should know, you would want to make sure the message was going only to him and not to RHETNT-L. The way to tell this is to first note in your header that the message comes from the list and not directly from Eric to you. Second, make sure that you address your reply to Eric by typing in his address at your e-mail program's TO: prompt.

5. Ending a Message

Always end a message with your name and e-mail address. As simple a rule as this is, people often forget it.

Since interfaces and e-mail programs vary so widely, you cannot always assume your e-mail address will automatically be visible to the person reading your message. If the message is sent directly to the person, this is less of an issue because he or she can usually rely on the Reply command to automatically send a message back to you. But there are times when for some reason the Reply command does not work and the person may need to double-check your address. It's always more convenient if he or she sees your address, so always close your message with it.

Signature Files

Many regular e-mail users create signature files. A signature file, sometimes called "sig" for short, is a file that contains at least your name and e-mail address. It is placed where your e-mail program can find it and is automatically appended to each message you write, thus assuring that you always end your messages with your name and e-mail address. Many signature files are more elaborate than just containing a name and e-mail address. They may also consist of home and work snail mail addresses, phone numbers (though we advise against this), a favorite quote, a disclaimer that the views expressed are the person's own and not his or her employer's, and ASCII art (pictures made from an arrangement of letters and characters). A good signature file works as effectively as a business card. However, signature files can become too elaborate and long. A good rule of thumb is to keep a signature file to five lines or fewer.

Here's what a signature file might look like.

```
* Nick Carbone          Marlboro College              *
* nickc@marlboro.edu     Marlboro, VT 05344            *
*                                                      *
* If you can touch your toes without bending your knees,   *
* you don't watch nearly enough TV.                    *
```

6. Using an Address Book

Each e-mail program will differ in how it creates, edits, and uses an address book, and whether it even calls the feature an address book. Elm, for example, calls this feature an "alias file." Eudora calls it "nicknames." An address book lets you create a shorthand for frequently used e-mail addresses so that you do not have to type in the full address every time you send a message. Nick exchanges mail with Eric once or twice a week; therefore, he's entered Eric's name and e-mail address in his alias file. When he writes to Eric, he uses the command for mailing, and when prompted for an e-mail address, he types **ec.** The e-mail program automatically adds wleric@showme.missouri.edu. Address books can also be used to include addresses for e-mail discussion lists. Furthermore, a group of addresses can be collected under one larger address to create a distribution list. For example, consider the following aliases in an address book:

Alias	Name of Person or List	E-Mail Address
rhet	Rhetnet	rhetnt-l@mizzou1.missouri.edu
ec	Eric Crump	wleric@showme.missouri.edu
nc	Nick Carbone	nickc@english.umass.edu
john	John Smith	j_smith@someplace.oit.edu
jane	Jane Doe	doe7789@someother.place.edu

You could create another alias that would address all of them at once. This is useful for group projects or, as one of our friends does, for keeping in touch with a far-flung family. Here's how it might look.

Alias	Name of Person or List	E-mail Address
edits	Editing Group	ec, nc, john, jane

A message addressed to "edits" would go to Eric, Nick, John, and Jane. Remember that to do this, you must first create an alias for each person. How each e-mail program handles the alias feature will vary, but it's one of the best features to learn how to use. In fact, most programs make it easy to use by providing a command or menu option, which, when selected, will prompt you for the information you need. In Elm, for example, to create the alias for Eric, Nick typed **n**, for new alias, and then had to fill in the following:

```
Enter alias name: ec
Enter last name for ec: Crump
Enter first name for ec: Eric
Enter optional comment for ec: Nice Guy
Enter address for ec: wleric@showme.missouri.edu
```

After filling in all this, he was asked:

```
Alias: Add a new alias to database...     Accept new alias? (y/n) y
New alias: ec is 'Eric Crump, Nice Guy'
Messages addressed as: wleric@showme.missouri.edu (Eric Crump)
```

By typing **y**, for yes, the alias was added. One final step particular to Elm was typing **e** to edit the alias list (an option that merely calls up the address book list file), and then pressing the **Ctrl** key plus the **x** key to save the update to the file.

Address books are the e-mail equivalent of speed dialing.

7. Saving Messages into Folders

Most e-mail programs allow you to sort messages into folders. For example, you might create a folder for each discussion list you are on. If you receive a message you wish to reply to later or save for some other reason, you can save it to a folder. When you use the folder system—and on most programs this is done by choosing the command to save the message—the program can be set, by going into an options or preferences menu, to suggest a folder name based on the name of the sender. Messages Nick receives from Eric are saved into a folder called wleric, the program's default name based on Eric's e-mail address, wleric@showme.missouri.edu. You can also choose a different name for a folder. For example, Nick has one folder called grammar where he saves messages that relate to the teaching of grammar.

8. Downloading and Uploading Files to Send by E-Mail

Downloading and uploading e-mail messages is most easily done by using ASCII, a standard for computer-generated characters, such as numbers, letters, and symbols. Most word processors will have a feature to save as text only. This option makes the text meet ASCII requirements so that it can be sent over e-mail by removing all formatting—bold, italics, underlining, set fonts— and saves your message as a plain text file. This allows the message to be sent and read in just about any word processor or e-mail program. There are other ways to send messages written in a program other than your e-mail program's text editor, but ASCII or text only is the easiest to learn.

Learn how to use the text only feature of whichever word processor you are using. But you should first experiment to see how the message reads after it is sent. You can do this by uploading a message and sending it to yourself.

Downloading and deleting messages are an important part of user netiquette. Cleaning your e-mail in-box makes sure your messages won't pile up and exceed the in-box's capacity. When your in-box is full, new messages will be rejected. Sometimes they will be sent back to the sender; sometimes they will get lost in cyberspace. In either case, you won't get the message. You will also tie up system resources. Each file takes up disk space, so many access providers limit each user to a fixed amount of space. This can be measured in total bytes, in total number of files, or in a combination of both. Regular housekeeping is one of the most important pieces of netiquette you can practice.

9. Dealing with Spam Messages

Spam in e-mail has nothing to do with the trademarked food product. Instead, it refers to a message that combines the worst aspects of telemarketing and door-to-door salespeople, or at least it feels that way when you receive it. Spam messages are indiscriminate intrusions into your e-mail, most often from a discussion list you may be on. Spammers like to target lists because the list does the work of spreading the message for them. Spam senders don't care that they are intruding into someone's e-mail; in fact, many secretly enjoy the mischief they cause. It's from this annoying and inane interruption that spam gets its name. The British comedy troupe Monty Python used to perform a recurring skit in which characters would burst out singing, "spam, spam, spam, spam, spam" over and over, bringing everything else going on in the skit to a stop.

Spams can often be identified from their subject lines: "Earn Big Money for Little Work," "1,500 Great Magazines." The easiest way to deal with spam is to simply delete the message and get on with your e-mail. Unfortunately, part of the spam phenomenon usually includes discussion of spam itself, which, in effect, increases the amount of spam. In other words, anyone can send spam to a discussion list, but only the list members can turn it into a prolonged nuisance by complaining on the list about it, turning spam into a kind of self-replicating spore.

10. Dealing with Flames

Generally, a flame is a message that makes an unfair attack or criticism on a person or a person's ideas. Sometimes messages not meant to be flames are taken as flames. At other times, people go out of their way to flame someone. Flames can involve the most vile and hateful language imaginable. The best thing to do if you think you've been flamed is to ignore it for a day and then respond without flaming, using patience, wit, and precision instead. If flames recur, simply ignore them. In e-mail, silence speaks volumes. If a writer asserts a position that you find abhorrent and cannot ignore, if your honor is at stake, then you should respond. But you should counter the position not by attacking it, but by asserting your own views and values. Take a positive stance, and write strongly on the issues you care about. Counter a flamer's arguments; never disparage his or her personality. Just be sure to address your views to the list; don't ever address a flamer more than once—you can't fight fire with gasoline.

CHAPTER 5

Mailing Lists: Hosts for Discussion Groups and Online Communities

CHAPTER CONTENTS
5.1 Introduction
5.2 How Mailing Lists Work
5.3 Mailing List Programs: Listserv, Listproc, and Majordomo
5.4 Finding Lists
5.5 Subscribing to Lists
5.6 Unsubscribing from Lists
5.7 Mail Options
5.8 Archives
5.9 Common Problems
5.10 Getting Help

5.1 Introduction

Electronic mail may seem almost magical when compared to its print-based predecessor, postal mail. It is astoundingly faster and more convenient (once you learn how to make it work). But even electronic mail by itself pales in comparison to the power unleashed by electronic mailing lists, which greatly expand the ability to communicate with others over the Net using e-mail.

5.2 How Mailing Lists Work

Mailing lists are like regular bulk mail except they are faster and more flexible. Bulk mail is often used when someone (usually an advertiser or sweepstakes organizer) wants to reach many people with the same information. They may obtain lists of street addresses and use them to scatter huge quantities of their material in the wind. E-mail lists operate much the same way. When someone sends a note addressed to the list's e-mail address, the mailing software "explodes" the note, sending a copy to every subscriber. Most mailing list software includes features for mail options, archive maintenance, and database searches. The basic list function is simple enough, however: distribute e-mail to e-mail addresses.

How Much Listspace Is on the Internet?

This simple question has a complicated answer. Thousands of mailing lists are on the Internet, perhaps 15,000 to 20,000, but that is only a guess. No one knows for sure how many there are because some are private (that is, not registered or indexed anywhere), and new ones are born every day. Few die. To give an example, in the fall of 1991, the University of Missouri-Columbia hosted about thirty-five public lists. As of the summer of 1995, it hosted 140, a 400 percent increase in less than 4 years. It's difficult to say whether this case is typical or not, but certainly the growth is impressive.

An Increasing Number of Lists

Probably the main reason the number of lists continues to grow is that mailing list software is so flexible. Mailing lists can serve a wide range of purposes. Some support small private working groups; some host open discussions on any topic; some provide a place for intensely focused debate on specific issues; some serve as places to exchange data; and some are used mainly to disseminate information. Lists are used by corporations, politicians, scholars, researchers, and students. They serve as a means of communication for committees, classes, electronic publications, fan clubs, and online communities. Some are very small, with only a handful of subscribers. Some are huge, for example, David Letterman's Top Ten List, TOPTEN@listserv.clark.Net, had 66,184 subscribers as of July 1995.

5.3 Mailing List Programs: Listserv, Listproc, and Majordomo

Perhaps dozens of different mailing list programs are available, but three are most common. Revised List Processor, usually referred to as Listserv, was developed by Eric Thomas and has long been the dominant mailing list program. It has been around since 1986 and recently became a commercial product supported by L-Soft International. Sophisticated and arguably the easiest of the three to use, Listserv became the most popular mailing list program during the heyday of BITNET (Because It's Time Network), a network that catered to academics and researchers who used lists to conduct scholarly discussions.

In the early 1990s, the Internet had clearly surpassed BITNET in both technology and popularity. Many institutions dropped their membership in BITNET and became Internet-only sites. That trend leveled the playing field for list software, and although L-Soft now offers Internet versions of Listserv, several Internet-based programs have since flourished. The most popular, Listprocessor, or Listproc, was developed by Anastasios Kotsikonas. Its popularity has been bolstered now that it is supported by the Corporation for Research and Educational Networking (CREN). Listproc is similar to Listserv in that it includes a range of features and is easy for subscribers to use. Listserv was developed for IBM mainframe computers that made up the heart of BITNET, but Listproc has always been an Internet-based program.

The third program, called Majordomo, was created by Brent Chapman. It is less commonly used (although gaining popularity), has fewer convenient features, and uses slightly different procedures. Whereas Listserv and Listproc have more features and are designed to handle large volumes of mail, Majordomo is a leaner program that is designed to support smaller lists.

For more information on mailing list software, see these web sites:

Listserv: http://www.lsoft.com/
Listproc: http://www.cren.net/www/listproc/listproc.html
Majordomo: http://www.greatcircle.com/majordomo/

For a Frequently Asked Question (FAQ) file by Norman Aleks that compares the major mailing list features, send e-mail to **listserv@listserv.net**. Leave the subject line blank, and in the first line type: **GET MLM-SOFT FAQ**.

5.4   Finding Lists

As the number of lists has grown, so has the number of list indexes. These are often referred to as "lists of lists" or "interest groups." Some are simple mailing list addresses, and some include brief descriptions of each list's purpose and subscription procedure. Even with the brief descriptions, though, the best way to discover what a list is like is to subscribe to see what kinds of conversations take place. It's an easy matter to unsubscribe if you find the list does not suit your purposes or address your interests.

Listserv Lists

Listserv, as far as we know, is the only mailing list program that is the subject of exclusive list indexes. That is, there are comprehensive indexes of public Listserv lists, but no similar indexes of Listproc or Majordomo lists. Because Listserv is the most commonly used mailing list program, indexes of its lists are generally good resources, especially for finding academically oriented lists. Here's how to find these lists of lists.

Via the Web

http://tile.net/tile/listserv/
http://www.liszt.com/

Via e-mail

Send e-mail to: listserv@listserv.Net
Leave the subject line blank.
Write: list global

This shows an entire index of Listserv lists—the document is nearly 7,000 lines long. To narrow the search, you can specify a topic by writing **list global/[topic]**.[1] Thus if you wanted to learn about literature lists, you would follow these directions, but you would change **list global** to **list global/literature.**

Interest Groups

The term *interest group* refers to indexes of mailing lists and sometimes USENET newsgroups. These are compiled according to subject, regardless of the software used to support the group. Interest group indexes are sometimes extremely large and often divided into a series of files. Here's where to find some interest groups.

Via the Web

    http://www.nova.edu/Inter-Links/cgi-bin/news-lists.pl
    http://www.mid.Net/DARTMOUTH/

Via Gopher

    Host: Gopher.es.Net
    Port: 70
    Path: O/pub/networking-info/interest-group.txt
    URL: gopher://Gopher.es.Net:70/00/pub/networking-info/interest-
    groups.txt
    Host: livia.unf.edu
    Port: 70
    Path: 1/computing/INTERNET/mailing-Lists
    URL:
    gopher://livia.unf.edu:70/11/computing/INTERNET/Mailing% 20Lists

5.5   Subscribing to Lists

The subscription process is very similar for most mailing list software, but keep in mind that although different programs share functions, they quite often have different ways of accomplishing

---

1. In all the examples for this chapter, do not type the [ ]that appear in the directions. These indicate a generic category in the command sequence. In this example, it would be the topic of your choice.

those functions. Think about the differences between popular word processors like Microsoft Word and WordPerfect. Both have similar functions and features for creating and formatting texts, but each has its own distinct way of doing those things.

> **NOTE:** One important feature of all mailing list software is that when you send a message to the software, you leave the subject line blank unless you receive specific directions to do otherwise.

This situation illustrates the difference between using networks to communicate with people and using them to communicate with machines. In most cases, when you subscribe, unsubscribe, or change mail settings, you are interacting with mailing list software, not with a human list manager. That means your message has to include very precise information. If one character is missing or out of place, the computer gets confused.

Subscribing in Listserv

Here is the Listserv command protocol.

Command	Comments
Send e-mail to: **listserv@host.domain**	host.domain is the address the list runs on.
Write: **subscribe [listname] Firstname Lastname**	You do not need your e-mail address; that will be read automatically by Listserv. Listserv is not case senstive.

For example, if John Milton wanted to subscribe to CREWRT-L, a list for creative writing, he would:

Send e-mail to: listserv@mizzou1.missouri.edu
Write: subscribe crewrt-l John Milton

If the list accepts public subscriptions, you'll automatically receive a welcome message with several basic Listserv commands, such as how to unsubscribe from that list. This message includes a suggestion that you keep the note for future reference. We recommend the same. The information may not seem necessary at the time, but when you need to unsubscribe from a list, it is embarrassing to have to ask. Even worse is sending an unsubscribe command to the list itself, which means that everyone on the list gets a copy of a message that only the mailing list program can process. This is a very common error. In fact, it is so common that some list members respond to it with scorn.

Some lists also maintain individualized welcome messages that come in addition to the default message from Listserv. It is a good idea to pay close attention to welcome messages because they often establish the purposes and conventions of the list. When you walk into a roomful of strangers, it's good to have an idea of their general perspective or political leanings; you should know where they're coming from. The same is true for joining a new e-mail list. A little attention at this point may save you some anguish and embarrassment later.

> **HELPFUL HINT:** Create a folder in your e-mail program for saving all list software messages. If you join a lot of lists, this will keep all the information you need for unsubscribing in one place. This folder will be especially helpful for those times when you will not have access to your e-mail—Christmas break, spring break, summer vacation. You'll find directions for putting list mail on hold until you get back.

Subscribing in Listproc

The procedures for subscribing to and unsubscribing from Listproc lists are identical to those for Listserv lists. The only eal difference is in the way you address the note to the mailing list program. Use **listproc@host.domain** rather than **list-**

serv@host.domain. For example, MegaByte University (MBU-L) is a list about computers and writing that uses Listproc. To join, John Milton would:

Send e-mail to: listproc@listserv.ttu.edu
Write: subscribe mbu-l John Milton

Notice that the list is called MegaByte University, but that the list name in the Listproc software database is MBU-L. If Milton writes: **subscribe MegaByte University John Milton,** he will receive an error message from Listproc@listserv.ttu.edu telling him there is no such list. Listproc, like Listserv, is not case sensitive, and will recognize either mbu-l or MBU-L.

Subscribing in Majordomo

Majordomo is slightly different from Listserv or Listproc in its subscription procedure. Of course, you would use **majordomo@host.domain** instead of **listserv** or **listproc.** However, in Majordomo, you do not include your name in the subscription command. You may optionally include your e-mail address, but that is not necessary. If you do include your name, Majordomo will put your name into its distribution list *instead* of your address. This will mean you will not get list messages because a message can't be mailed to a name; it must go to an e-mail address.

Send e-mail to: **majordomo@host.domain**
Write: **subscribe [listname]**

or

Write: **subscribe [listname] [user@host.domain]**

TechNoCulture (TNC) is a Majordomo list. If Jane Austen wanted to subscribe to it, she would:

Send e-mail to: majordomo@ucet.ufl.edu
Write: subscribe tnc

or

Write: subscribe tnc jane@dead.novelists.com

5.6   Unsubscribing from Lists

Unsubscribing from Listserv

To leave a Listserv list:

> Send e-mail to: **listserv@host.domain**
> Write: **signoff [listname]**
> or
>
> Write: **unsubscribe [listname]**

Note that unlike the subscribe command, your name is not included. In fact, if you do include your name, the program will be unable to process the command. For example, if John Milton wanted to unsubscribe from CREWRT-L, he would:

> Send e-mail to: listserv@mizzou1.missouri.edu
> Write: signoff crewrt-l

On unsubscribing, you will get an automatically generated acknowledgment message, but this one isn't worth saving. It just says you are unsubscribed. You can delete this message and, if you like, the messages you received when you first subscribed. Since you are no longer associated with the list, you do not need to keep copies of Listserv messages. If you subscribe again at another time, you will automatically get a new set of messages.

Unsubscribing from Listproc

The procedure is identical to Listserv, but again use **listproc** rather than **listserv** in the address. For John Milton to unsubscribe from MBU-L, he would:

> Send e-mail to: listproc@listserv.ttu.edu
> Write: signoff mbu-l

Unsubscribing from Majordomo

To unsubscribe from Majordomo, the procedure is:

> Send e-mail to: **majordomo@host.domain**
>
> Write: **unsubscribe [listname]**

or

Write: **unsubscribe [listname] [user@host.domain]**

For example, if Jane Austen wanted to unsubscribe from TNC, she would:

Send e-mail to: majordomo@ucet.ufl.edu
Write: unsubscribe tnc
or

Write: unsubscribe tnc jane@dead.novelists.com

5.7 Mail Options

Lists can generate great quantities of e-mail. Even lists that are normally docile may go wild on occasion if a particularly controversial subject comes up. The first reaction many people have is acute exasperation. They are often tempted to quickly unsubscribe to stop the relentless tide of mail. However, if you have compelling reasons to stay with a busy list, it's worth learning how to manage the volume.

The simplest and perhaps best approach may be the liberal use of the Delete key. Some people initially feel that deleting messages is rude, an act similar to ignoring someone in face-to-face situations. Of course, no one is likely to know (unless you tell) whether you've deleted any particular message. Besides, it's an accepted practice. Most experienced list subscribers have adapted their reading habits to fit the situation. They "skim and dive," running their eyes quickly over the first part of each note, sometimes getting no further than the subject or sender lines before deciding about whether to read further. They delete often and without hesitation. And it's OK.

Listserv Mail Options

Several mail options are also available with Listserv. The main options are NOMAIL, MAIL, DIGEST, and INDEX. To use them, you would:

Send e-mail to: **listserv@host.domain**
Write: **set [listname] [option]**

NOMAIL tells Listserv to stop the flow of mail but to keep you as a member of the list. MAIL tells Listserv to resume sending mail. A typical use for this command, in addition to taking occasional breaks from the mail flood, is to stop mail during vacations. To set CREWRT-L to NOMAIL:

> Send e-mail to: listserv@mizzou1.missouri.edu
> Write: set crewrt-l nomail
> To begin receiving mail again:

> Write: set crewrt-l mail

DIGEST tells Listserv to bundle all the mail for each twenty-four-hour period and send it as a single (often very *big*) message. To change mail delivery to DIGEST:

> Send e-mail to: listserv@mizzou1.missouri.edu
> Write: set crewrt-l digest

> To begin receiving mail in non-DIGEST form again:

> Write: set crewrt-l nodigest

INDEX tells Listserv to send a single message every day that lists all the notes distributed by the list during the day, along with instructions about how to retrieve only those messages you wish to read. To do this:

> Send e-mail to: listserv@mizzou1.missouri.edu
> Write: set crewrt-l index

To begin receiving each mail message directly again:

> Write: set crewrt-l noindex

To see what your current mail settings are on a Listserv list:

> Send e-mail to: **listserv@host.domain**
> Write: **query [listname]**

To query CREWRT-L:

> Send e-mail to: listserv@mizzou1.missouri.edu
> Write: query crewrt-l

Eric's query to CREWRT-L returned this:

Subscription options for Eric Crump [wleric@SHOWME.MISSOURI.EDU], listCREWRT-L:

MAIL	You are sent individual postings as they are received
FULLHDR	Full (normal) mail headers (formerly "FULLBSMTP")
REPRO	You receive a copy of your own postings
NOACK	No acknowledgment of successfully processed postings

Had Eric set his subscription to DIGEST or INDEX, those options would have been mentioned in the Listserv response instead of MAIL.

Listproc Mail Options

Listproc's mail option commands are slightly different from Listserv's. Rather than NOMAIL, Listproc uses POSTPONE. Listproc, like Listserv, has a DIGEST feature, but it does not have an INDEX feature. The protocol for Listproc is to:

Send e-mail to: **listproc@host.domain**
Write: **set [listname] mail [option]**

To POSTPONE mail from MBU-L:

Send e-mail to: listproc@listserv.ttu.edu
Write: set mbu-l mail postpone

To resume mail from MBU-L:

Write: set mbu-l mail ack

To DIGEST mail from MBU-L:

Send e-mail to: listproc@listserv.ttu.edu
Write: set mbu-l mail digest

To return to normal mail delivery:

Write: set mbu-l mail ack

To check your current mail settings on a Listproc list:

Send e-mail to: **listproc@host.domain**
Write: **set [listname]**

Notice that the word *mail* is not needed as part of the command structure. To run this command for MBU-L:

Send e-mail to: listproc@listserv.ttu.edu
Write: set mbu-l

Here's what Eric's subscription on MBU-L sent back after he checked his mail settings:

Current settings are:
ADDRESS = WLERIC@SHOWME.MISSOURI.EDU
MAIL = ACK
PASSWORD = xxxxxxxx
CONCEAL = NO

Majordomo Mail Options

Majordomo does not currently support the mail options offered by Listserv and Listproc.

5.8 Archives

The majority of public lists are archived, meaning a copy of each note is stored somewhere, usually on the same computer where the list resides. It can be important to know if a list is archived and how to access the archive files. Since most students have limited storage space on their e-mail accounts, it's not practical to save every note that might come in handy some day—especially when those notes are already being stored elsewhere.

Listserv Achives

To see if Listserv lists are archived:

Send e-mail to: **listserv@host.domain**
Write: **index [listname]**

If no archive exists for the list, Listserv returns a brief note saying the index file is not known. The command **index wcentr-l** returned the following message:

File 'WCENTR- L FILELIST' is unknown to LISTSERV

If we wanted to see whether CREWRT-L was archived, we would send mail to listserv@mizzou1.missouri.edu with the command **index crewrt-l.**

The resulting note indicates that CREWRT-L is archived and that the files are compiled weekly. An excerpt from the reply Listserv sent about CREWRT-L follows. It shows the files for June 1994. (These are no longer available by the way; archives are kept only for the most recent six months at the University of Missouri. So although archives are useful, you should check with those lists that are archived to learn how long messages will be saved.) In the excerpt you see a list of "logs," files that contain all the messages written in the week indicated by the "started on" date.

```
*
*  NOTEBOOK archives for the list
*  (Weekly notebook)
*                          rec           last - change
* filename filetype   GET PUT -fm lrecl nrecs   date      time  Remarks
* -------- --------   --- --- --- ----- -----  --------  -------- -------------------------
  CREWRT-L LOG9406A   ALL OWN V     80  7143 94/06/07 22:54:40
Started on Wed, 1 Jun 1994 00:05:03 -0600
  CREWRT-L LOG9406B   ALL OWN V     80  9477 94/06/14 22:57:08
Started on Wed, 8 Jun 1994 04:43:12 -0500
  CREWRT-L LOG9406C   ALL OWN V     80 10424 94/06/21
18:18:51 Started on Wed, 15 Jun 1994 00:09:01 -0500
  CREWRT-L LOG9406D   ALL OWN V     80 10766 94/06/28
23:54:12 Started on Tue, 21 Jun 1994 22:25:44 -0700
  CREWRT-L LOG9406E   ALL OWN V     80  4760 94/06/30 23:46:09
Started on Tue, 28 Jun 1994 22:28:04 -0700
```

Each of the files can be obtained from Listserv using the **get** command. For instance, to get the file from the third week of June:

Send e-mail to: listserv@mizzou1.missouri.edu
Write: get crewrt-l log9406c

The file we would receive is large—10,424 lines long—so it might be more efficient to use a database search command. This command searches the archive by topic and e-mails those messages to you.

Like all the commands covered so far, the **database search** command is sent as e-mail to the host machine on which the list runs. It's more complex than the get or set commands shown earlier, so we're including a template for you to use. Type it into a file exactly as it appears so that you can insert it into an e-mail message to Listserv.

```
//ListSrch JOB Echo=no
Database Search DD=Rules OUTLIM=2000 f=mail
//Rules DD *
Search [keyword] IN [listname]
index #.4 date.8 sender.30 subject.35
print

// EOJ
```

If, for instance, you were studying contemporary poetry and wanted to see if anyone on CREWRT-L was familiar with the work of Allen Ginsberg, you could search the archives with this command:

```
Send e-mail to: listserv@mizzou1.missouri.edu
Write:
//ListSrch JOB Echo=no
Database Search DD=Rules OUTLIM=2000 f=mail
//Rules DD *
Search ginsberg IN crewrt-l
index #.4 date.8 sender.30 subject.35
print
/*
// EOJ
```

The result from Listserv includes both an index *and* the full text of the messages (if there are any) that contain the keyword you searched for. In the preceding example, Listserv returned:[2]

```
> Search ginsberg IN crewrt-l since 01-jul
--> Database CREWRT-L, 7 hits.

> index #.4 date.8 sender.30 subject.35
```

2. We deleted the text of the e-mail messages from the index listed here.

#	DATE	SENDER	SUBJECT
2853+	95/07/05	DANNYANGEL@DELPHI.COM	Some thoughts
2936+	95/07/18	gmcvay1@OSF1.GMU.EDU	Prose poem book
2941+	95/07/18	OLUND@VAX2.WINONA.MSUS.EDU	Naropa/ Crewmeeting
2999+	95/07/24	jlyon@CARBON.CUDENVER.EDU	Re: Orv's Naropa Experience
3001+	95/07/24	jlyon@CARBON.CUDENVER.EDU	Re: Orv's Naropa Experience
3001+	95/07/24	vhicks@MAIL.WIN.ORG	Re: Orv's Naropa Experience
3001+	95/07/24	john.oughton@SHERIDANC.ON.CA	Re: Orv's Naropa Experience

Listproc Archives

The **index** command also works to determine whether a Listproc list is archived. Here's how the command would be used for MBU-L:

> Send e-mail to: listproc@e=/listserv.ttu.edu
> Write: index mbu-l

Here's the reply from Listproc:

> Archive: mbu-l (path: mbu-l) -- Files:
>   about (0 part bytes) -- list mbu-l 1 0
> /cwis/server/listproc6.0c/archives/mbu-
>   9406 (1 part, 201273 bytes)
>   9407 (1 part, 1301745 bytes)
>   9408 (1 part, 1118577 bytes)
>   9409 (1 part, 1343300 bytes)

The message tells you that the files are stored on the host domain in the path indicated in the first line(Listserv.ttu.edu in this example). This is not information you need to be concerned with. This archive is collected monthly; thus 9406 indicates June 1994. The message also tells you the file is in one part and that it contains 201273 bytes, or about 201K. This is what you want to know.

To receive the file for June 1994, you would:

Send e-mail to: listproc@listserv.ttu.edu
Write: get mbu-l 9406

With Listproc, you cannot do the kind of database search that you can with Listserv.

Majordomo Archives

The index command produces the same basic results with Majordomo lists, but the message has a different look. For example:

Send e-mail to: majordomo@ucet.ufl.edu
Write: index tnc

The response looks like this:

```
>>>> index tnc
total 152
-rw-rw-r--   1 daemon   majordom   77299 Jun 27 00:26 archive
```

The filename, archive, is at the end of the last line. The total indicates the number of messages in the file (152) and -rw-rw-r-- shows the file attributes. You also learn that it is a Majordomo file of 77299 bytes and that it was last updated on June 27 at twenty-six minutes after noon.

To retrieve the archive file:

Send e-mail to: majordomo@ucet.ufl.edu
Write: get tnc archive

Web and Gopher Archives

Mailing list archives can be made available via the Web or Gopher (a menu-based, text-only program), as well as via e-mail. Web archives are especially convenient to use since they are easy to search and sort.

Gopher is generally easier to use than e-mail or FTP (File Transfer Protocol) to obtain archive files. An example of a gopher archive is at

Host: gopher.missouri.edu
Port: 70
Path: 1/campus/archives/WWC-1
Web URL: gopher://gopher.missouri.edu:70/11/campus/
archives/WWC-1

These are the archives for the Writing With Computers list at the
University of Missouri.

A new kind of archive for the Web is done with Hypermail.
Hypermail collects the messages from a list and puts them into
a web page. Those who visit the web page can then directly
respond to a message via its e-mail address. Cybermind, a discussion list about cyberspace, maintains a Hypermail archive that
can be accessed from The Cybermind Homepage
(http://www.portal.com/~spartan/). The following screenshot is
of The Cybermind Hypermail archive for December 1995.

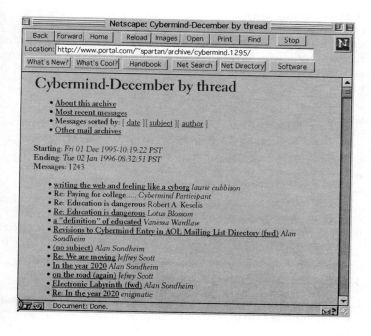

For more information about Hypermail, see:
http://www.eit.com/software/hypermail/hypermail.html.

5.9 Common Problems

Mailing list software is powerful, whether you're using the sophisticated Listserv or the simpler Majordomo, but it is also stupid.
New users can often become frustrated because they believe they
are following procedures exactly, but the list software refuses to
understand their commands. Like most commonly used software,
mailing list programs are capable of responding to precise commands only. Anything even slightly different is completely unrec-
ognizable.

One Wrong Character

Screens can be difficult to read, especially when you are trying to
distinguish between similar characters. For example, it's not
unusual for people, when trying to subscribe to CREWRT-L, to
type **mizzoul** (with lower-case L) rather than **mizzou1** (with number one) in the host name. The numer one looks very similar to
lowercase L.

Right Syntax, Wrong Program

Although the differences between mailing list programs are generally slight, those slight differences might as well be vast chasms
when it comes to software "comprehension." Speak Listservese to
Listproc and the program will stare at you blankly. When in
doubt about the exact command syntax, send a one-word command to Listproc (or Listserv or Majordomo): help. The basic help
message includes instructions on how to get help files on specific commands.

Talking to the Wrong People

One of the most common errors made on the Net is posting mailing list commands to lists. That is, messages that are meant for the
software to process are sent to the people who are subscribed to

the list. With the exception of the list owner, there's nothing those people can do with the command—except get annoyed at the person who sent it for cluttering their mail in-boxes with junk. Always remember to address commands to the software—Listserv, Listproc, Majordomo, or whatever program you're trying to communicate with—not to the list.

Unintentional Masquerading

This problem is rarely caused by users and can usually be fixed by contacting list owners. When you subscribe to lists, the software picks up your address from the header of the subscription message. The mailing list uses that address to identify you as a subscriber. If you send a message from another address, even a very similar one, the program cannot recognize you as being you. Being off by one character or word is all it takes. Even though the addresses may look as though they belong to the same person, from the mailing list's perspective, geoff.chaucer@canterbury.edu is an entirely different user from geoff.chaucer@miller.canterbury.edu.

5.10 Getting Help

Before you get to the point of utter frustration with a list-related problem, contact the list owner and ask for assistance. Nearly all list owners are volunteers. They start and maintain lists because they think the venue provides a service to a specific community of people with interests similar to theirs. Part of their responsibility is to help people who run into problems subscribing, signing off, or changing subscription settings.

Like any frustrating situation, it's tempting to get some of that anger and anxiety off your chest. Be careful, though, not to direct your frustration at the person who's in a position to help you. List owners, for instance, are often as frustrated as subscribers by the strange and inscrutable problems that pop up on the Net. They are your allies, not your opponents. They can often help you quickly solve a problem. Try to explain in as much detail as you can exactly what you tried to do and what the result was. It's always a good idea to write down any error messages you receive. Even if they make no sense to you, they might make sense to someone with more experience and help him or her deduce the solution.

To find the e-mail address of a Listserv list owner:

Send e-mail to: **listserv@host.domain**
Write: **review [listname] short**

For CREWRT-L:

Send e-mail to: listserv@mizzou1.missouri.edu
Write: review crewrt-l short

You will receive a file of information about the list, including the owner information. Here's the excerpt of how this information appears for CREWRT-L. Notice that the owners are clearly identified:

```
Owner= wleric@showme.missouri.edu  (Eric Crump)
Owner= flynnm@softint.com  (Matt Flynn)
Owner= PALMER@stmarytx.edu  (Palmer Hall)
Owner= olsen@cobber.cord.edu  (Scott Olsen)
```

To find the owner of a Listproc list:

Send e-mail to: **listproc@host.domain**
Write: **review [listname]**

For MBU-L:

Send e-mail to: listproc@listserv.ttu.edu
Write: review mbu-l

When you get your reply, look for the address in the cc: line of the header that comes at the top of the message sent to you by Listproc:

```
From: listproc@listserv.ttu.edu
To: wleric@showme.missouri.edu
Cc: nobody@listserv.ttu.edu
Subject: REVIEW MBU-L
```

Any queries you need to make to the owner of MBU-L can be addressed to nobody@listserv.ttu.edu.

To find the appropriate address for a Majordomo list:

Send e-mail to: **majordomo@host.domain**
Write: **info [listname]**

For TNC (TechNoCulture):

Send e-mail to: majordomo@ucet.ufl.edu
Write: info tnc

As part of the reply, you will find this:

> If you have problems using Majordomo, or if you need help on a matter unrelated to the mailing lists, please direct your questions to "system@ucet.ufl.edu".

CHAPTER

Telnetting on the Internet

CHAPTER CONTENTS
6.1 Introduction
6.2 Connecting to a Telnet Database

6.1 Introduction

Telnet is the protocol used to connect your computer to another on the Internet. You are most likely to use it in one of two ways. You have to log into your Internet account, and at the account prompt, type the command **Telnet** and an address. Or you have to have access to a computer on campus that has a dedicated Telnet connection. (A dedicated connection is a cable connection between your computer and the host computer.) With these you can choose a Telnet icon from your desktop; you will then receive a dialog box asking you to type in the domain address you wish to reach.

Once you reach the other computer by Telnet, you may have to log into it. A few Telnet addresses will connect you to an automatic login; others will give you the login name and password; and still others will require you to know in advance the login name and password to use.

> **HELPFUL HINT:** Telnet is useful for reaching your own account when you are away from your campus. If you visit a friend at another school, you can access your computer through your friend's. After he or she logs on, Telnet to your campus computer. When you are prompted for a login and password, use the same ones you use at your campus. For this to work, you need to know the Telnet address for your campus.

6.2 **Connecting to a Telnet Database**

The best way to understand Telnet is to think of it as *tele*phoning on the Inter*net*. In the following example, you will dial Harvard's Online Library Information Service (HOLLIS) to access the Educational Resources Information Center (ERIC) database.

At the prompt (in this example, prompt%) type:

prompt%**telnet 128.103.151.247 3006**

where:

telnet = the command—typing it is akin to picking up a phone receiver and poising your fingers over the numbers. Note the command is in lowercase.
128.103.151.247 = the number you want to connect to—it's the Internet number for Harvard's library
3006 = the extension (or port) for the ERIC database

Note that there is no space between the prompt and the start of the command. You must have a space between telnet and the number, as well as between the address number and the extension you are trying to reach. Further, since this example takes place in a UNIX operating system, the command is typed in lowercase.

Because you are working from a prompt line and not a menu system, you will need to hit the Enter key after each command.
After a few moments, the following appears:

Trying
Connected to 128.103.151.247.
Escape character is ^.

HOLLIS Plus
Now connecting to HOLLIS

To leave this resource hold down the control key (Ctrl) and press x.
(^X)

This information scrolls by with only a short pause. The following screen then appears:

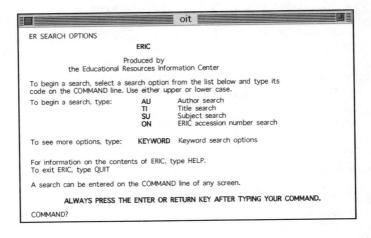

Typing **su**, a command you are sending from your keyboard through the Telnet connection to HOLLIS, gets you to the following screen:

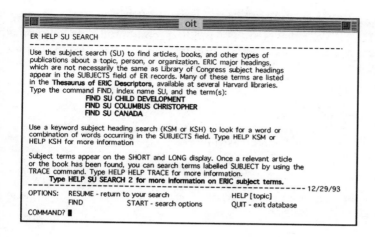

The command **su shakespeare** gives the following result:

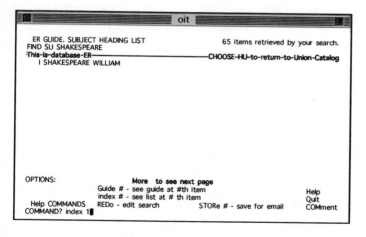

As you can see from the sequence of screen snapshots, the Telnet interface is text only. In this example, you connected directly to an online database. The commands you typed at the computer activated a program stored at Harvard's library. With a little practice, you can get comfortable using Telnet in a number of different interfaces. The important thing to remember is that while in Telnet your keyboard is sending commands to a distant computer. To see another example of a Telnet session, go to Chapters 11 and 12.

HELPFUL HINT: Because you are sending a signal over a longer distance, you will sometimes experience lag time while using Telnet. Lag time means that you have to wait a bit for your signal to reach the computer and for the computer to send the signal back to your screen. Lag time can be aggravated by Telnetting at peak hours (8 a.m. to 5 p.m., Monday through Friday) or if the host computer (the computer you reach) or application is being heavily used.

CHAPTER 7

Gopher and Lynx

CHAPTER CONTENTS
7.1 Introduction
7.2 Bookmarking
7.3 Advanced Navigating: Direct Addresses
7.4 Saving
7.5 Downloading Files with Gopher and Lynx
7.6 Searching for Resources in Gopher and Lynx
7.7 Gopher Commands
7.8 Lynx Commands

7.1 Introduction

Gopher and Lynx are both text-based tools for navigating the Internet. Gopher is used to navigate Gopher menus and directories, sometimes referred to as gopherspace. Lynx is used to navigate the World Wide Web. The descriptions and examples in this section are for users who must use a modem or its equivalent to connect to a mainframe or campus server and log into that remote computer. This procedure makes the user's computer a terminal of the server; it means the user can run Gopher and Lynx from his or her own keyboard by sending commands over the phone line. This type of connection means any graphic, audio, moving picture, or software files must be downloaded to the user's own computer before opening them up. During a Gopher or Lynx session, only text (or ASCII) files can be viewed.

Gopher

Gopher is a menu-driven interface that automates connections by creating links to other computers on the Internet, bringing a user to particular data or programs on those computers. Gopher can also incorporate Telnet and File Transfer Protocol (FTP) in its structure. However, the World Wide Web (WWW) is fast becoming the navigational tool of choice since it can access and run Gopher servers and all of their connections as well as just about any other Internet software. Many sites have ceased upgrading their Gopher servers and are instead dedicating their resources and support to the WWW. Still, this transition is not evenly paced, and Gopher remains an important and vibrant Internet tool.

Lynx

Lynx is perhaps the most popular text-based software for browsing on the World Wide Web. Its main advantage over graphic browsers (see Chapter 10) is speed. Lynx does not have to wait for graphics to load because it cannot show them. Moreover, for those who do not have a direct connection to the Internet and who cannot afford the faster modems and software needed to get a high-speed phone connection, Lynx offers a quick, reliable way to navigate the Web. Lynx can be reached, if your school carries it, by dialing into your account and typing **lynx** at your account prompt.

The one drawback to Lynx is that more and more web sites are being designed and coded for optimal use with Netscape's most advanced graphical browser. These new sites can be disordered and confusing to read in Lynx; at worst, they are inaccessible. For example, if you visit Disney's Toy Story web page (http://www.toystory.com/) with Lynx, you will find that it uses what is called an image map. An image map takes a graphic image and assigns links to different parts of the image. For Toy Story, the image map might be a photo of all the characters in the movie, and clicking one of them leads to information. However, this requires a visitor to have a graphic browser so that he or she can call up the links that are embedded, and thus available only from the page's graphic images. But don't be discouraged by the occasional high-tech site; many thoughtful web designers include Lynx friendly versions of their pages.

Some Brief Words on Navigating

Navigating in Gopher and Lynx is simply a matter of using the arrow keys on your keyboard to move the cursor. In both Gopher and Lynx, the cursor moves among links. The down arrow moves you down, the up arrow moves you up. To choose a link, press the right arrow. To exit a choice and move back to the previous screen, press the left arrow. The Enter key can also be used to select a link the cursor is on.

Note that in Gopher, however, you move among menu items; in Lynx, you move up and down a page with links in it. Gopher uses numbers to itemize its menus; in Lynx, an active link will be in boldface on your screen. Also when in Lynx, the up and down arrows will automatically move from link to link.

> **HELPFUL HINT:** The first thing you should do when you begin using Gopher or Lynx (or any other new Internet tool) is play. Walk through the command lists at the end of this chapter—it will help you get used to the interface.

7.2 Bookmarking

A bookmark is probably the most immediately useful command to know when working in either Gopher or Lynx. Since Gopher and Lynx are founded on built-in connections called links, you can easily find yourself going from link to link as you explore. When you come to a web page or Gopher directory that you like, and that you may want to return to later, it's easier to bookmark that site than it is to remember the path—the series of links you followed—that got you there. A bookmark, instead of recalling the path, takes you directly to the site. Thus with a bookmark, all of your favorite sites are just one link away.

Bookmarking in Gopher

Most Gopher servers can be entered by typing the command **gopher** at your account prompt.

Using bookmarks in Gopher is very simple. Here are the commands you will need:

a   Add selected menu item to bookmarks
A   Add current directory and its entire menu to bookmarks
v   View bookmarks
d   Delete a bookmark entry

Typing **A** saves a Gopher directory that you are already viewing, not one that you can still select. Consider the following Gopher page as an example. If you type **A**, the menu you see will be saved to your bookmark file. If you type **a**, the menu choices under 13. News, Jobs, and Other Timely Information/ will be saved because that's where the cursor is. You can see what is under the menu before you, but you don't know yet what is under number 13.

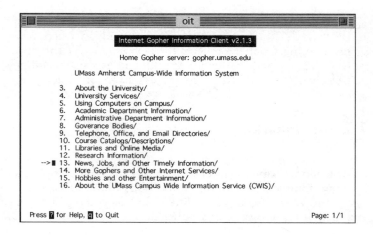

In Gopher, your bookmark page will also be a numbered list. Once your bookmark page is up, it can be navigated by scrolling with your cursor or by typing the number you wish to view.

Notice that Gopher uses a numbered menu system to present information. A slash (/) at the end of a menu entry means that the menu leads to more information—there may be links to more directories or files. If a gopher item does not end with a slash, then you have reached a single file. If it is a text file, then you can read it.

Bookmarking in Lynx

The bookmark commands for Lynx are similar to those for Gopher. To return to a Lynx page without having to repeat all the links you made, you can use the following bookmark commands:

a   Add the current link to your bookmark file
v   View your bookmark collections

When you type **a** to add the bookmark, you'll be asked if you want to add the **d**)ocument, **l**)ink, or **c**)ancel. Typing **d** will add the page you are on and all its links. Typing **l** will add whatever link your cursor is on.

Here's what a Lynx page looks like; this sample is from the Alliance for Computers and Writing homepage (http://english.ttu.edu/acw/), one of the most useful Internet resources for writing.

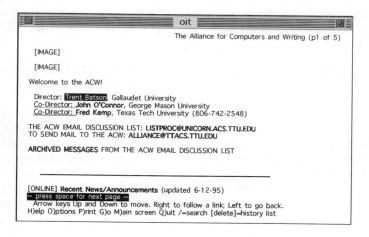

Note that the link for Trent Batson is highlighted. This means that if you chose l (for link) when prompted for what you want in your bookmark file, you would not get the ACW homepage, but the link to Trent Batson, which, in this case, brings you his full address and a command that allows you to send him an e-mail message. (That's right, with the World Wide Web, you can send e-mail.)

Notice also that segments of the page show the word [*IMAGE*] on them. If you are viewing this page with a graphic browser, you will see a picture or graphic instead of [IMAGE].

7.3 Advanced Navigating: Direct Addresses

Sometimes you will have a direct address and path, perhaps from a work-cited entry found in someone's bibliography or from an e-mail message telling you of a good resource. In these cases, you will want to open a direct connection instead of searching through a number of menus.

Gopher and Direct Addresses

Gopher navigation with a direct address is a little complicated until you get used to it. A Gopher address must be put in three parts instead of one stream, as it is in the Web (see the section "Lynx and Direct Addresses"). If you look at the following work-cited entry, you'll see that a Gopher address has three parts: the host, the port, and the path you select (which we call "select" for short).

> Sill, David. "Laser." The ACRONYMs Dictionary. 15 February 1993. Internet. Gopher: info.mcc.ac.uk, port: 70, select: 1/miscellany/ acronyms.

When citing or following up on sources in gopherspace, you need to know two things: how to learn what the parts are (for citing), and how and where to type in the parts (for linking). Here's how to discover the host, port, and path. The Gopher menu that *The ACRONYMs Dictionary* is on looks like this:

```
Internet Gopher Information Client v2.1.3
info.mcc.ac.uk

—> 1. About the acronym dictionary
    2. Acronym dictionary (keyword search) <?>

Press ? for Help, q to Quit, u to go up a menu          Page: 1/1
```

To get the necessary information for a citation, you type the ^ command. (That is, you simultaneously press the Shift key and the number 6 to get a caret.) After typing the command, the following information will appear on your screen:

```
Type=1
Name=ACRONYMs dictionary
Path=1/miscellany/acronyms
Host=info.mcc.ac.uk
Port=70
<URL:gopher://info.mcc.ac.uk:70/11/miscellany/acronyms>
```

Notice that you also get the information as it would appear in a URL (Uniform Resource Locator—the name for the protocol, host, and path you need to locate a resource) for a web site address. You should also note the variations in the address parts:

Web Addresses	**Gopher Addresses**
Host and port combined:	Host and port separate:
info.mcc.ac.uk:70/	Host: info.mcc.ac.uk
	Port: 70
Path: 11/miscellany/acronyms (note the extra 1)	Path: 1/miscellany/acronyms

To go to this Gopher site via the Web, you would type the URL as one continuous line, with the slashes, as it appears in the link information. To open this link in Gopher, you must fill in the separate lines of the dialog box that will pop up over your current menu when you type the command o to open a link. Here's what that will look like:

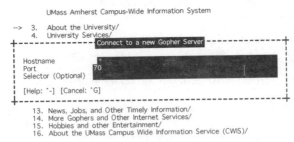

In the Gopher dialog box, the port is defaulted to 70. Nine times out of ten, you will not need to change it. The dialog box tells you that you have chosen to "Connect to a new Gopher Server"; the hostname address takes you to the first menu in the new server. This menu is also referred to as the main menu or root menu for the new Gopher server's site because other menus grow or extend from it. The link to the dictionary is two directories, or menu choices, away from the main menu. By including the path information in the selector field, you automatically select the menu options that will take you to *The ACRONYMs Dictionary.* Thus to open a link directly to *The ACRONYMs Dictionary,* you would fill in the lines in the dialog box like this:

hostname: **info.mcc.ac.uk**
port: **70**
selector (optional): **1/miscellany/acronyms.**

The selector is optional because you do not need to fill it in to complete a link to the new server; you need it only to go beyond the new server's main menu into a submenu. By the way, you can tell the host in this example is in the United Kingdom because of the .uk extension on the address. If you recall the citation we used as the basis of this demonstration, we used the term *select* (short for selector) instead of the term *path.* People following one of your citations will most likely want to open a link, so it is helpful to have the citation closely correspond to the open dialog box.

Lynx and Direct Addresses

In Lynx, and the Web in general, it is easy to type in addresses that take you directly to a homepage; in fact, it is encouraged. You may have noticed that many television and magazine advertisements now include web addresses. For example, we found the Disney address for Toy Story at the end of a television ad for the movie. As you begin to use e-mail, you will find that more and more people will include their homepage's URL.

To use one of these addresses in Lynx, type **g** (for go to.) On the bottom of your screen, just above Lynx's help menu, you'll be asked for a URL. Always type in the full URL exactly as it appears in the source you got it from.

HELPFUL HINT: If you type in a URL or Gopher path and you end up with a failed connection, one trick that sometimes works is to try the connection again, only with less information. Thus if the URL http://www.marlboro.edu/~nickc/vrpr/vrpr.html (a link to a course on writing on the Internet taught by Nick at Marlboro College) failed, you could try http://www.marlboro.edu/ (a link to the Marlboro homepage). This will allow you to see if there's a link from the homepage to the source you were trying to reach. In Gopher, the equivalent would be leaving the select option blank. You can experiment with how much of the address to leave off the end. Often, addresses undergo slight changes—perhaps a file is moved or slightly renamed. A return to the source can sometimes salvage the search.

7.4 Saving

Saving a File in Gopher

When you find a file you want to save, type **s** (for save). To save a file, you need to be in it. Typing **s** will open a dialog box that offers a name for the file—the name that the person who put the file online gave it—but you can change it. If the filename is very long, you might want to change it since shorter names mean fewer opportunities for error.

If you want to mail a file from Gopher, you can do so while you are in the file by typing **m**. You'll get a dialog box asking for an e-mail address. All you have to do is type one in and press

Enter. If you type **m** while you are at a Gopher menu and not reading an actual file, you will be asked if you wish to return to the main menu.

Saving a File in Lynx

To save in Lynx, you need to type **p** (for print). Just think of it as printing to a file rather than to a printer.

After typing **p**, a page appears that shows you the following:

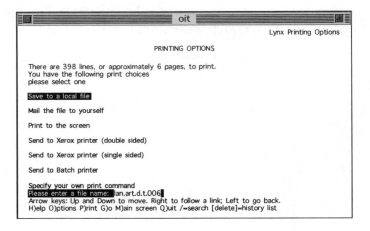

If you choose to save to a local file (as we did in the screen snapshot), a filename will appear at the bottom of your Lynx page. As in Gopher, you can change the name. If you choose to e-mail the file to yourself, the same location on the page will ask you to input an e-mail address; you can write in your own e-mail address.

> **HELPFUL HINT:** In Lynx, if you send a file by mail, the program will automatically include the URL, which is the World Wide Web address another user would need to find the same source you did. This is a useful way of saving documents that you might want to use in a research paper, and for noting the URL for your works-cited entry. It's best to e-mail yourself the page in order to ensure an accurate URL.

7.5   Downloading Files with Gopher and Lynx

How you download files will depend on how you are connected to the Internet and what software you are using. Once you save a file to your account, the method for downloading it will be the same whether the file comes from an e-mail message or from an essay you accessed in Gopher or Lynx. The only difference in download procedures will be determining whether files are text files, binary files, or, for Macintosh users, MacBinary files. For each variation, you need to let your communications and downloading software know which kind of file you are downloading.

Binary files include software files, graphics files, audio files, and video files. Text files will usually be in ASCII, which you recall is a way of saving files so that they loose all formatting associated with any word processing programs, including bold, italics, font choices, margins, and other features. With ASCII, all you get is text; word processors will usually have a Save As option under the File menu called Text Only. That is their version of ASCII. Sometimes you will receive (or send) a word processing file that you do not want converted to ASCII because it is important to keep the formatting. In these instances, the file will be binary and will usually be compressed. You will have to have the correct software on your computer to read it.

PPP (Point to Point Protocol) and SLIP (Serial Line Internet Protocol) connections effectively put your computer directly on the Internet. They often come with software that helps automate downloading, such as Fetch. If you don't have these kinds of connections, and many users do not, then you need to know how to download files with a dial-in modem connection that uses a regular phone line. To do that, you need to know the following:

1. Whether the file you will download is ASCII, binary, or MacBinary.
2. The types of downloading protocols (or methods) your modem communication software will support: xmodem, ymodem, zmodem, or kermit are common ones.
3. The types of downloading protocols the server you reach by modem will support.
4. How to match the protocols and file types. You need to set your communications software to receive a file the same way you are going to command the server to send it. If you tell

your school's server to send a file as ASCII using zmodem, you must set your communication software to receive as ASCII, zmodem.
5. If you want to upload, you need to know how to reverse the process.

7.6   Searching for Resources in Gopher and Lynx

Both Gopher and Lynx have software that allows you to search the WWW or gopherspace by using keywords. In Gopher, the main search engine for gopherspace is Veronica; however, Gopher also has a search engine for FTP (File Transfer Protocol) sites called Archie. Veronica can be accessed by typing **o** (for open)—which is used to open a direct connection in Gopher—and, in the dialog box, typing **gopher.tc.umn.edu** where it asks for a path. Once you arrive at the menu—University of Minnesota's Gopher—choose **8. Other Gopher and Information Servers/**. This menu choice will have a link to Archie as well as other databases.

In Lynx, a number of search tools are available. These are cited in detail in the resources compendium in Part Four of this book.

7.7   Gopher Commands

Remember that Gopher commands are always case sensitive. An **a** command is different from an **A** command.

Navigating

Right Arrow, Enter	Select menu item cursor is on
Left arrow, u	Go back one menu
Down arrow	Move to next line in menu
Up arrow	Move to previous line
>, +, PgDn, space	View next page
<, -, PgUp, b	View previous page
Type a menu number	Go to a specific menu number
m	Go back to the main menu

Bookmarking

a   Add menu number the cursor is on to the bookmark list
A   Add current directory or menu you are in to the book-
         mark list
v   View bookmark list
d   Delete bookmark menu entry cursor is on

Other

q   Quit with prompt
Q   Quit unconditionally
s   Save current item to a file
S   Save current menu listing to a file
D   Download a file
r   Go to root menu of current item
R   Go to root menu of current menu
=   Display link details about current item
^   Display link details about current directory
o   Open a new Gopher server
O   Change options
/   Search for an item in the menu
n   Find next search item
g   "Gripe," via e-mail, to administrator of current item

7.8 Lynx Commands

Remember that all Lynx commands are in lowercase.

Navigating

Down arrow   Highlight next topic
Up arrow   Highlight previous topic
Right arrow, Enter   Jump to highlighted topic
Left arrow   Return to previous topic
+ (or **space**)   Scroll down to next page
- (or **b**)   Scroll up to previous page
? (or **h**)   Help (this screen)
a   Add the current link to your bookmark
                            file
c   Send a comment to the document
                            owner
d   Download the current link

e	Edit the current file
g	Go to a user-specified URL or file
i	Show an index of documents
j	Execute a jump operation
k	Show a list of key mappings
m	Return to main screen
o	Set your options
p	Print to a file, mail, printers, or other
q	Quit (Q for quick quit)
/	Search for a string within the current document
s	Enter a search string for an external search
n	Go to the next search string
v	View your bookmark file
z	Cancel transfer in progress
Backspace	Go to the history page
=	Show file and link info
\	Toggle document to show html coding
!	Spawn your default shell
Ctrl-R	Reload current file and refresh the screen
Ctrl-W	Refresh the screen
Ctrl-U	Erase input line
Ctrl-G	Cancel input or transfer

CHAPTER 8

File Transfer Protocol

CHAPTER CONTENTS
8.1 Introduction
8.2 Anonymous FTP

8.1 Introduction

File Transfer Protocol (FTP) is an Internet procedure used to get a file from a remote computer on the Internet and have it sent to the computer from which you issue the FTP command. If you connect to your Internet account with a modem to a server and type the FTP command at the prompt, the transferred file will be saved to your account space on the server. To move the file to the computer on your desk is another step. If you have a direct access or

PPP/SLIP (Point to Point Protocol/Serial Line Internet Protocol) connection that allows you to use an automated FTP program such as Fetch, the file will be placed directly onto your personal computer.

8.2 Anonymous FTP

A number of Internet computers host anonymous FTP sites. Anonymous FTP allows outside users to log in as a guest and retrieve files stored on the host's computer. Since accessing these files is akin to someone leaving the backdoor unlocked and the porch light on, it is courteous to keep the following in mind:

1. If possible, FTP at a time when the host machine is not likely to be busy.
2. As a login name, use the word *anonymous*.
3. When asked for a password or identification, type in your e-mail address. This allows the site managers to have a sense of where users are coming from. Of course, it ceases to make you anonymous in the strict sense of the word. Anonymous in this sense does not mean privacy; it's like having a guest pass.

The following example—an FTP session to the University of Kansas public FTP archives to retrieve a copy of Lynx—is based on using a UNIX platform reached by dialing in from a modem. Note that the commands are written in lowercase because UNIX is a case-sensitive operating system. In this example, prompt% is the name of the starting system's UNIX server; commands entered are in bold; explanatory notes are in roman.

The example features the use of the following commands:

ftp [address]	Initiates an FTP connection from a command line prompt.
anonymous	The username for logging into publicly available archives.
ls or dir	Lists files and other directories in the current directory of an FTP server.
cd [directory name]	Changes directories into the named directory.

cdup   Changes up to a previous directory. This
                        makes sense as a concept if you think of
                        each directory you enter as moving you
                        farther down a directory tree.

get [file name]   Transfers a file to the computer from
                        which you began the FTP session.

quit   Ends an FTP session; this will close the
                        connection and return you to your own
                        command line prompt.

prompt%ftp **ftp2.cc.ukans.edu**
Trying 129.237.33.1

Connected to ukanaix.cc.ukans.edu.
220 ukanaix.cc.ukans.edu FTP server
(Version 4.9 Thu Sep 2 20:35:07 CDT 1993) ready.

Name (FTP2.cc.ukans.edu:nickc): **anonymous**
331 Guest login ok, send ident as password.

Password:

When you type the password, you will not see the letters on
your screen. This is a security feature of computer passwords used
to keep people from learning your password by looking over your
shoulder.

230 Guest login ok, access restrictions apply.

After completing the login, a prompt appears. The next series
of commands are used to navigate the FTP directories at the site.

FTP> ls

This command lists files and directories. Note that the screen
gives a lot of information, including that the command suc-
ceeded.

200 PORT command successful.

This indicates the **ls** command was received and is in progress.

150 Opening data connection for /bin/ls.

This indicates the data for the command will be accessed.

bin
etc
lib
pub
usr
226 Transfer complete.
25 bytes received in 0.0039 second (6.3 Kbytes/s)

List of directories; note that this information is sandwiched between FTP progress messages. FTP messages always begin witha number.

FTP> cd pub/WWW/Lynx

The **cd** command stands for change directory. In the example, we move three directories at once, into pub, into WWW (a directory within the pub directory), and then into Lynx (a directory within the WWW directory). We could move one directory at a time as well. The first time you visit a site, you may want to just learn your way around. Unless you have directions indicating otherwise, most visits to an FTP site will begin with the pub, for public access, directory. After completing the command, the following message appears:

250 CWD command successful.

FTP>**ls**

While in the pub/WWW/Lynx directory, the **ls** command reveals the files and folders listed. Files will often have extensions such as tar.Z, which indicate the compression format used to make the file take up less space on the disk; however, often does not mean always (note the file called README at the top of page 81).

200 PORT command successful.
150 Opening data connection for /bin/ls.

README
freeWAIS-0.202.tar.Z
Lynx2-2
Lynx2-3
Lynx2-3-7
Lynx2-4
Lynx2-4-1
Lynx2html.tar.Z
Lynx_help_files.tar.Z
Lynx_help_files.zip
mailcap
mime.types
226 Transfer complete.
161 bytes received in 0.0039 second (40 Kbytes/s)

FTP> cd Lynx2-4-1

250 CWD command successful.

You can see that all names have file compression format extensions. (To save space, archives are compressed by special software that cuts down the file's number of bytes.) Instead of typing **cd Lynx2-4-1** as above, we first tried **get Lynx2-4-1** and received a message that Lynx2-4-1 was not a file, but a directory. We mention this because you will likely make the same mistake at some point. When you do, just know that instead of **get,** you will want to use **cd.**

FTP> ls

200 PORT command successful.
150 Opening data connection for /bin/ls.
Lynx2-4-1.aix32.exe.Z
Lynx2-4-1.linux-ncurses.exe.Z
Lynx2-4-1.osf.exe.Z
Lynx2-4-1.tar.Z
Lynx2-4-1.zip
226 Transfer complete.
107 bytes received in 0.0078 seconds (13 Kbytes/s)

FTP> get Lynx2-4-1.zip

The **get** command is used to actually transfer the file to the computer from which the FTP session was launched. It is important to type the filename exactly as it appears in the directory listing.

200 PORT command successful.
150 Opening data connection for Lynx2-4-1.zip (727242 bytes).
226 Transfer complete.
local: Lynx2-4-1.zip remote: Lynx2-4-1.zip
729978 bytes received in 1.302 seconds (5.4 Kbytes/s)

FTP> cdup

The **cdup** command moves you back one directory at a time. We need to use it in this example to go back to the directory where the Lynx help files are stored.

250 CWD command successful.

FTP> get Lynx_help_files.zip

200 PORT command successful.
150 Opening data connection for Lynx_help_files.zip (57449 bytes).
226 Transfer complete.
local: Lynx_help_files.zip remote: Lynx_help_files.zip
57654 bytes received in 7.4 seconds (7.6 Kbytes/s)

FTP> quit

221 Goodbye.

Since these files are compacted with zip compression software, all we need to do in this case is unzip them. (Zip software specializes in archiving. A "zipped" file uses half the space as an unzipped file.) Back on our own computer, we type the command to unzip the files. Of course, before you can do this, you need to make sure the computer you use has the unzip software. As you see in the next command line, you type the command name followed by the name of the file. After you do this, you will see a list of separate files. Compression software can also take many files and put them into one file for easier transfer among computers.

```
prompt%unzip Lynx2-4-1.zip
```

After completing this command, you will find a number of files to use in setting up Lynx, including directions. However, before installing any software on your account, check to see if you need it (Lynx may already be available.) and if you have permission to install it on the server. See Chapter 11 for a full example of how to unzip a file.

CHAPTER 9

Getting Freeware and Shareware from Public Archives

CHAPTER CONTENTS
9.1 Introduction
9.2 Freeware
9.3 Shareware
9.4 Downloading
9.5 Macintosh Decompression Utilities
9.6 Windows Decompression Utilities
9.7 Common Sites for Freeware and Shareware
9.8 How to FTP Freeware and Shareware for Macs and PCs

9.1 Introduction

One of the features of the Internet that may surprise new users is its overriding spirit of cooperation. One example of this is the software programs developed by individuals and businesses that are stored in archives anyone can access. Users can browse the archives and select the software they'd like to try.

The archives are usually provided by universities that have significant storage space. The archives contain all manner of software, including various utility programs, games, educational programs, and communications programs.

9.2 Freeware

Software labeled freeware is simply there for the taking. An example of freeware is Disinfectant, a Macintosh antivirus program created by John Norstad. He and his colleagues not only make the program available free of charge, but every time a new Macintosh virus appears, they quickly revise the program to account for the new threat. They very often release a new version of Disinfectant within a few days of the discovery of a new virus.

> **HELPFUL HINT:** You should make sure you have up-to-date virus detection software on your computer. Viruses are programs that wreak havoc in computers. Sometimes they are casual pranks, but other times they are highly destructive. Use protection software whenever you download an Internet file from an archive.

9.3 Shareware

Software labeled shareware comes with a price, almost always a modest price, and can be downloaded by anyone. No bills or invoices arrive by postal mail, however. Each transaction is based on the honor system. If you download a shareware program and like it enough to keep using it, you're expected to send the author his or her asking price, which is usually between $5 and $25 per copy. Shareware programs sometimes come with just the address of the developer, which may be displayed during the program's startup process. Or they may come with a registration form ready to print and mail in.

9.4 Downloading

Most archives are stored on machines running UNIX systems, and they are tapped by using File Transfer Protocol (FTP). You can also reach software archives through Gopher or the World Wide Web. One excellent WWW resource is http://www.shareware.com/ a page that allows users to search several archives at once.

In Gopher, you can type the o command to open a connection. At the prompt for the path name, type **gopher.archive.merit.edu**, and you will arrive at the Merit Gopher menu. From there, choose **6. Merit Software Archives/** to get the following menu:

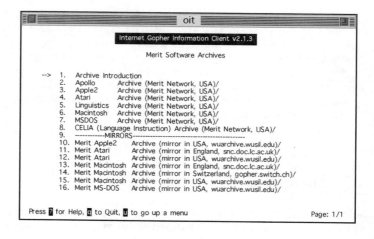

Just to give you a hint of how much software is available at this one archive, we'll show you what's in menu item 6, Macintosh (See the screen on page 87).

With Gopher, you simply work through the menu until you find the software you want. As you can see from the combination of files and links listed in the above menu, there's much to choose from. The Merit Archive can also be accessed on WWW URL:via gopher://gopher.archive.merit.edu:70/11/. software-archives.

When accessing software, you will notice that it is compressed so that it does not take up as much space and downloads faster. Since a compressed file often contains more than one file, it helps to think of it as a packed suitcase. Decompressing unpacks the suitcase and lets you use what's inside. When shareware and freeware are stored in archives, they are put into individual files by compression software that encodes and packs them. By packing many files and lots of data into one suitcase, it becomes easier for the software to travel.

However, this means that you will need some way to decompress the software before you can use it. If you are lucky, you have access that will automate the decompression for you. The exact procedure for downloading and unpacking software to a personal computer can vary quite a bit depending on the capabilities of your system.

```
            Macintosh   Archive (Merit Network, USA)

  1.  00help            contains    10 files /
  2.  00introduction    96-01-06    21K
  3.  00ls - lRfile     96-01-17    52K
  4.  00newfiles        contains    256 files 1 link(s)/
  5.  development       contains    367 files /
  6.  game              contains    760 files /
  7.  graphics          contains    240 files /
  8.  hypercard         contains    571 files /
  9.  misc              contains    795 files 3 link(s)/
 10.  powermac          contains    238 files /
 11.  sound             contains    194 files /
 12.  sytem.extensions  contains    1858 files /
 13.  util              contains    1566 files 5 link(s)/
```

9.5 Macintosh Decompression Utilities

Once a freeware or shareware file is on your machine, you need to run decompression and decoding utilities to render it ready to use. Those utilities are often available from college computing services departments, or they can be purchased. Many archived programs are now compressed in "self-extracting archives" (noted by the use of .sea as the extension after the filename). Those files do not require any additional utility programs in order to decompress and decode them. However you would do well to get a good decompression software program. One very good one, available for both Macintosh and PC formats, is StuffIt Expander, from Aladdin Systems (http://www.aladdinsys.com/).

As the folks at Aladdin note on the homepage for StuffIt, one of the problems with downloading decompression software for Macintoshes is that you need decompression software to decompress the decompression software. Chicken and egg indeed! StuffIt Expander is Aladdin's Freeware software for expanding files compressed for the Macintosh. It can expand StuffIt files (.sit), BinHex files (.hqx), MacBinary files (.bin), and Compact Pro files (.cpt).   Because you need software to unpack the software, the URL http://www.aladdinsys.com/obstufex.htm gives you details on a number of ways to solve this problem, including checking online services such as America Online and eWorld. If none of the suggestions look as though they will work for you, you can query Aladdin by e-mail at cust.service@aladdinsys.com. In your subject heading, you should write Query Freeware StuffIt Expander. In your e-mail, explain that you are interested in a copy of their freeware version of StuffIt Expander, but cannot access a decompressed copy. They'll let you know how to order an unpacked version for the cost of a diskette and shipping and handling.

9.6 Windows Decompression Utilities

Aladdin also makes a version of StuffIt that will run on Windows. If you go to URL http://www.aladdinsys.com/#SFP, you'll find a link to the version for Windows. It comes as a Windows executable file. (Executable files use an .exe extension and are used for running programs.) All you have to do is download it to your computer, and it is ready to run. Make sure you set your communications software to download the file as binary and not text. Follow the directions in Windows for adding new software, and you'll be all set to go. StuffIt Expander for Windows will decompress the following file types: StuffIt (.sit), ZIP (.zip), uuencoded (.uue), BinHex (.hqx), MacBinary (.bin), ARC (.arc), Arj (.arj), and gzip (.gz).

HELPFUL HINT: Note that the Windows version will decompress Macintosh formats. With newer model Power Macintoshes, disks formatted for PCs can be read by Macs. If you have a friend with Windows, and you use Macintosh, you can download Stuffit Expander on Windows, set it up, and then use that to decompress StuffIt Expander for your Macintosh.

9.7 Common Sites for Freeware and Shareware

Macintosh Software Archives

INFO-Mac

Because of the persistently heavy load on Stanford's INFO-Mac archive, its maintainers recommend that people try to use nearby "mirrors" of their site instead. The mirror sites, like a mirror image, contain identical copies of the files located at the Stanford University INFO-Mac home site. Some of the sites in the United States that mirror Stanford University's INFO-Mac archives follow.

INFO-Mac Mirrors

University of Florida, Gainesville, Florida
   FTP://FTP.circa.ufl.edu/pub/software/ufmug/mirrors/Info-mac/

University of Hawaii, Honolulu, Hawaii
   FTP://FTP.hawaii.edu/mirrors/info-mac/

University of Illinois at Urbana-Champaign, Urbana, Illinois
   FTP://uiarchive.cso.uiuc.edu/pub/systems/mac/info-mac/
   http://uiarchive.cso.uiuc.edu/

University of Iowa, Iowa City, Iowa
   Telnet://grind.isca.uiowa.edu/mac/infomac/
   FTP://grind.isca.uiowa.edu/mac/infomac/

MIT Laboratory for Computer Science, Cambridge, Massachusetts
   http://hyperarchive.lcs.mit.edu/HyperArchive.html

Washington University, St. Louis, Missouri
  FTP://wuarchive.wustl.edu/systems/mac/info-mac/
  http://wuarchive.wustl.edu/systems/mac/info-mac/
  Gopher://wuarchive.wustl.edu/11/systems/mac/info-mac/
  fsp://wuarchive.wustl.edu/systems/mac/info-mac/
  nfs://wuarchive.wustl.edu/archive/systems/mac/info-mac/

The GLOBE at Cornell University, Ithaca, New York
  http://globe1.csuglab.cornell.edu/

Oregon State University, Corvallis, Oregon
  FTP://FTP.orst.edu/pub/systems/info-mac/

University of Michigan, Ann Arbor, Michigan
  http://www.umich.edu/~archive/mac/

Windows and DOS Software Archives

California State University-San Marcos, San Marcos, California
  http://coyote.csusm.edu/cwis/winworld/winworld.html

Greater Flint Educational Consortium
(TUCOWS: The Ultimate Collection of Winsock Software)
  http://GFECnet.gmi.edu/Software/

Windows and DOS Software Mirrors

Northern Indiana Internet Access, Inc.
  http://www.niia.Net/tucows/

Solar Eclipse Information Services
  http://www.seis.com/~tucows/

The Genesee Free-Net
  http://gfn1.genesee.freenet.org/tucows/

OAK Software Repository (Oakland University)
  http://www.acs.oakland.edu/oak/oak.html

For more Mac and PC shareware sites, see Jim Knopf's "Father of Shareware" Web page at: http://www.halcyon.com/knopf/jim.

9.8 How to FTP Freeware and Shareware for Macs and PCs

If you prefer to access freeware and shareware written for Macintosh or PC operating systems by FTP instead of using a Gopher or WWW access, and if you do not have a connection enabling you to use an automated program such as Fetch, then the following FTP examples will be helpful. In Chapter 8, we showed you the basics of FTP. In that chapter, we used an example where we got a copy of a UNIX-based program; we FTPed from a UNIX workstation, and everything was straightforward. The following examples have a few wrinkles you need to know about when you FTP for software to use on your own computer.

The following example shows what the Washington University archives would look like if you were looking for Macintosh freeware and shareware. WU's archive contains mirrors of a number of big FTP sites. The archive itself is one of the most popular and most important FTP servers on the Internet.

> **HELPFUL HINT:**   Note that many FTP servers provide a welcome message or message of the day (MOD). These messages sometimes contain important information about using the site, so it's worth giving them a glance.

```
prompt> ftp wuarchive.wustl.edu
Connected to wuarchive.wustl.edu.
220 wuarchive.wustl.edu FTP server (Version wu-2.4(3) Tue Aug 8
15:35:34
CDT 1995) r.

Name (wuarchive.wustl.edu:wleric): anonymous
331 Guest login ok, send your complete e-mail address as password.
Password:

230- If your FTP client crashes or hangs shortly after login please try
230- using a dash (-) as the first character of your password. This will
230- turn off the informational messages that may be confusing
230- your FTP client.
230- This system may be used 24 hours a day, 7 days a week. The
230- local time is Wed Aug 30 23:12:56 1995. You are user number
230- 299 out of a possible 300. All transfers to and from wuarchive
230- are logged. If you don't like this then disconnect now!
230 Guest login ok, access restrictions apply.
```

Failed Connection Messages

Many software archives are popular spots, but the machines they reside on do not have limitless capacity for simultaneous logins. Usually when you try to login as "anonymous" and the connection fails, it's because the machine is too busy to handle any more users. Here is what the Washington University FTP server's too busy message looks like:

Name (wuarchive.wustl.edu:wleric): **anonymous**
530- Sorry, there are too many anonymous FTP users using the
530- system at this time. Please try again in a few minutes.
530-
530- There is currently a limit of 300 anonymous users. Yes, there
530- REALLY are that many users on wuarchive—this message is not
530 the result of a bug. User anonymous access denied.
Login failed.

If the FTP server is busy, it rejects the anonymous login right away and doesn't waste your time requesting your e-mail address as a password.

Getting Software Files

If you're using a UNIX or other general-use system like VM/CMS (Virtual Machine/Conversational Monitor System) or VMS (Digital Equipment Corporation's operating system), you will need to change the file type to binary, and then type the command **get** followed by the exact filename as it appears in the directory. You do this by typing an **i** before you type **get.** This step is crucial for downloading from a UNIX, VM/CMS, or VMS workstation to either a Macintosh or PC. Here is an example of changing directories and getting a file, in this case, to get to the INFO-Mac archive directory to access virus detection software. We take you through the steps of changing directories and finding the file wanted. Note that the command to change the file to binary is used just before issuing the **get** command. The purpose is to make sure both systems agree on the file type. Remember, binary files are programs, images, audio, and formatted text files.

You've logged in and got your bearings at the Washington University FTP server, and now you are ready to go to their INFO-Mac archives.

FTP> cd info-mac
250 CWD command successful.

FTP> dir

The **dir** command is an alternative to **ls**. Not all servers will
support both; you may have to try one or the other. Like **ls**, **dir**
will list everything in the directory.

200 PORT command successful.
150 Opening ASCII mode data connection for /bin/ls.
total 143
lrwxrwxrwx 1 root   archive 22 Mar 8 23:29 00readme.txt
                                    ->help/about-art
drwxr-xr-x 26 root   archive 1024 Jun 6 02:48 Old
lrwxrwxrwx 1 root   archive 3 May 23 23:16 _Anti-Virus -> vir
lrwxrwxrwx 1 root   archive 3 May 23 23:16 _Application ->
                                    app
lrwxrwxrwx 1 root   archive 3 May 30 00:03 _Art_&_Info -> art

For brevity's sake, we have deleted the middle portion of this list—
it takes up nearly a page.

drwxr-xr-x 2 root   archive 12288 Aug 21 04:55 rec
drwxr-xr-x 2 root   archive 9728 Aug 21 04:55 sci
drwxr-xr-x 3 root   archive 11264 Aug 20 03:47 snd
drwxr-xr-x 4 root   archive 8192 Aug 20 03:38 text
drwxr-xr-x 2 root   archive 1024 Aug 20 03:46 vir
226 Transfer complete.

FTP> cd vir
250 CWD command successful.

You can tell this is a directory you can go into because the line
begins with drwxr-xr-x. The initial d in the string is the directory
indicator.

FTP> dir
200 PORT command successful.

```
150 Opening ASCII mode data connection for /bin/ls.
total 997
-rw-r—r—  1 root   wheel   214490 Apr 7 21:38 disinfectant-36.hqx
-r—r—r—  1 root   archive 322288 Nov 13 1993 gatekeeper-130.hqx
```

Once again, many files were listed. We've deleted from this example about thirty others for the sake of space.

```
226 Transfer complete.
```

```
FTP> i
200 Type set to I.
```

The **i** command sets the transfer mode as binary, which is necessary to preserve the program's integrity.

```
FTP> get disinfectant-36.hqx
200 PORT command successful.
150 Opening ASCII mode data connection for disinfectant-36.hqx
226 (214490 bytes). Transfer complete.
217810 bytes received in 422.3 seconds (0.5037 Kbytes/s)
local: disinfectant-36.hqx remote: disinfectant-36.hqx
```

```
FTP>quit
```

Variations

One complicating factor in the process can be local file naming conventions. UNIX allows long filenames, but some systems have narrow limitations. VM/CMS, for instance, requires filenames in two words, neither of which can be longer than eight characters. So, CMS users will have to create new filenames to match their system since UNIX filenames do not match the CMS naming convention.

In previous examples, you simply saw the **get** command followed by the filename exactly as it appears in the FTP server's directory listing. Here, in order to rename the file so that it will be accepted on the CMS operating system, the new filename is added to the command string. The protocol is **get exactfilename newfile.name.** A period in the new filename will show up as a space on the CMS system, thus putting the filename into two words. Here's how the command looks:

```
FTP>get disinfectant-36.hqx disinfec.hqx
```

The file will appear in a CMS user's file list as DISINFEC HQX. Note that the user wisely chose to keep the BinHex extension (.hqx) as part of the new filename. That will help remind him or her that the file is software and must be downloaded in binary format.

CHAPTER 10

Graphic Browsers

CHAPTER CONTENTS
10.1 Introduction
10.2 Netscape
10.3 Mosaic
10.4 MacWeb and WinWeb
10.5 A Selection of URLs to Explore

10.1 Introduction

Graphic browsers are credited with spurring much of the World Wide Web's recent rise in popularity. Soon after the release of Mosaic, developed by the National Center for Supercomputer Applications at the University of Illinois, use of the Web began a dramatic rise that continues today. And in a circular relationship, the rapid growth of the Web inspires more graphic browsers. The Web's growth will probably level off at some point, but for the immediate future, graphic access to the Web is going to be an exciting ride.

Graphic browsers differ from the original text-only browsers in that they not only have a graphic interface—users of Macintosh and Microsoft Windows operating systems are familiar with graphic interfaces, with their windows, icons, buttons, and menus—but can also display graphic images, including photographs, animations, and video. Most graphic browsers today don't actually play sound and display video, but they facilitate the process by opening "helper applications." For instance, if you select a link to a video clip, your web browser will look in your computer's directories for a program that can display video. Many Macintosh users have a program called Sparkle, which browsers will recognize and launch when they encounter video clips. Sparkle then shows the clip the browser has downloaded.

The situation is changing fast, though, and by the time this book is released, browsers will likely be much more sophisticated than they are now. Java, a new programming language recently released by Sun Microsystems, is even now redefining what the Web is and does. Browsers are incorporating Java capability by using HotJava, a Java interpreter. Java will allow small application programs, called "applets," to be downloaded with documents, providing whatever functions—animation, video, audio—are required by the writers of the document. That means the days of helper applications like Sparkle may be numbered. Necessary applications will be delivered over the Net rather than residing on users' machines. That new capability is expected to change the Web dramatically. See http://www.javasoft.com/index.html for more information.

In this chapter, we will cover some basic information about three graphic browsers: Netscape, Mosaic, and MacWeb/WinWeb. Netscape is the most popular and arguably the best of the freely available browsers. Mosaic, still a popular and stable product, was the first graphic browser to capture the attention of the Internet community. MacWeb and WinWeb use less computing resources, so they are popular among people who do not have high-end machines and connections to the Net.

10.2 Netscape

Introduction

Netscape provides the fastest and glitziest access to the Web. Current reports indicate that it holds about 75 percent of the

browser market. Whether this number is accurate or not, few people dispute that it is the most popular web browser. Netscape
Communications Corporation, creator of the Netscape browser,
develops secure World Wide Web browsers for business and government. The company also provides browsers at no charge for
educational use.

Netscape tends to be assertive about developing features that
include new HyperText Markup Language (HTML) functions.
(HTML is the coding used to create web pages.) As a result,
Netscape generates a certain amount of controversy in the Web
community because the enhancements often are not yet accepted
parts of the current standard, which means they will not work if
the same page is viewed through another browser. As a particularly notorious example, Netscape introduced a feature that lets web
page designers make particular words or phrases blink. No other
browser supports the <blink></blink> tag (the term tag refers to
instructions the browser follows when presenting a document;
they are invisible to viewers of the document), so if someone looks
at a page with blinking text in it via MacWeb, for instance, the
words will appear as they do normally, not as blinking.

Netscape continues to grow in popularity in part because its
enhancements give more control over page appearance to HTML
authors, allowing them to change font size, add color, animate
images, and so on. One of the new features of Netscape 2.0 is
something called "frames." These allow web page authors to create separate windows within the browser's main window. The
author can then design pages so that new documents can appear

within those inner windows. It is a feature that has web developers very excited. Netscape also tends to be faster than most other graphic browsers because it can open up more than one connection to a server at once. That means it can download text and graphic files at the same time, putting pieces of a page together simultaneously rather than sequentially. Other browsers may load text first, then each image file in turn.

Netscape 1.1N for the Macintosh takes up about 1.4MB of disk space and requires at least 3MB of RAM to run.

Netscape Built-In Features

Graphic browsers generally include built-in features to help you get around the sometimes confusing world of the Web. Two of the most helpful are the Bookmark (or Hotlist) feature and the History feature, both of which help you keep track of where you've been.

Bookmark

Netscape's Bookmark feature is a menu listing sites you've visited that you may wish to visit again. It is a user-extendible list of web sites. When you find an interesting page, go to the Bookmarks menu and choose Add bookmark. Netscape also allows you to rearrange bookmarks and organize them under different headers by using the View bookmarks option.

History

Netscape's History feature is found under the Go menu. It keeps track of all the places you visit during your current session. If you decide you want to return to a site you visited previously, you can choose it from the Go menu rather than using the Back button to retrace your steps one page at a time. Netscape also has directory buttons and a directory menu that contain links to various resources provided by the company, including links to its pages. This feature can be handy for finding out more information about the browser itself and its capabilities.

Show Location

This option, found under the Options menu, is not activated when you first start Netscape, but it is convenient to have it available. If you activate the Show location option, you get a narrow box near the top of the window that shows the URL of your current location. This feature will help you get the correct URL for when you need to cite for a research paper. Into that box you can also type or paste URLs that you want to visit.

Default Page

Graphic browsers give users the freedom to choose any starting location, meaning the web page that automatically appears every time you start the program. This is known as the default page. Netscape comes with its starting point set at Netscape Communications' homepage. One problem with leaving this as the default page is that Netscape's servers are sometimes busy, so when you start you may get an error message saying the server you chose is not available. It's generally a good idea to change the default to a web page you are likely to use regularly. Ideally, you should set a web page on your computer so that the starting place is always available. One possibility is to set a simple page that contains a list of frequently visited URLs, a kind of page-based hotlist or bookmarks list.

To change the default location, first go to the page you want to have as your starting location. If the page is located at a remote location, choose Open Location from the File menu. If the page is located on your own computer, choose Open File from the File menu. Select the URL in the location box, copy it, then go to the Options menu and select Preferences. In Preferences, there is a category, which usually appears by default, called windows and link styles. In that dialog box there is a box for the Homepage URL. Paste in the URL you copied. Close Preferences by selecting the OK button.

Other Interface Elements

When you start using any browser, it's probably a good idea to keep all its elements in view so that you know at a glance what your options and possibilities are. However, as you become more familiar with the Netscape's interface, you may wish to display more window space. Netscape also lets you toggle the toolbar, locations, and directory buttons, making them visible or hidden whenever you wish. For example, if your connection to the Net is slow or unstable, you may want to turn off Auto Image Load, under the Options menu. Images take much longer to download than text, even under good conditions. If connection conditions are poor, image loading can make browsing the Web a slow, frustrating experience.

E-Mail

One very convenient feature of sophisticated graphic browsers like Netscape is their ability to serve as communication as well as information tools. You can send e-mail from within Netscape as long as the preferences file includes your mail server and e-mail address. If you select a link on a web page created by the <mailto:user@host> tag (commonly used by web page maintainers as a convenient way for readers to provide feedback about the contents of their pages), Netscape will automatically give you the mail feature. E-mail can be used at any time, however, whether a mail to link is available or not. It is often used to e-mail the contents of a page to someone who does not have access to the Web or to send a URL to someone who you think might be interested in a site you've discovered. To do so, choose Mail document from the File menu.

To enter your server and e-mail address, select Preferences from the Options menu, then select the Mail and news option. There, you will find four boxes to fill out: Mail (SMTP) server, Your name, Your e-mail, and Organization. Fill out the boxes completely, but the most important ones are Mail (SMTP) server and Your e-mail. The mail server entry is likely to be whatever is to the right of the @ symbol in your e-mail address (that's not always the case, so it might be a good idea to check with local computing service people to verify the correct setting). In Eric's case, he would type **showme.missouri.edu** in the Mail server box and **wleric@showme.missouri.edu** in the E-mail box.

Netnews

Netscape serves as a fairly sophisticated news reader. If you wish to read USENET newsgroups, or Netnews, via Netscape, the browser offers many of the features found on programs designed specifically as news readers. To use the Netnews feature, go to the Mail and News section of the preferences, and enter the address of a Netnews server. If you aren't sure of the Netnews server address at your school, check with your computer support center.

View Source

One of the best ways to learn how to create your own web pages is to study the pages already on the Web. Many graphic browsers have a feature called View Source, which launches a text editor to display the HTML used to create the page you see with the browser. This feature lets you compare what a page looks like with its underlying structure in HTML. In Netscape, the View Source feature can be found in the View menu on the menu bar. If you select Document source, Netscape will look for a text editor, launch it, and use it to display the HTML for the current web page. The program designated to launch when View Source is chosen can be changed in the Options preferences. You may prefer to use a word processor or another text editor. The information can then be saved or printed for future reference.

It's common practice to borrow structural and design elements from web pages. HTML seen under the View Source feature is sometimes used as a template for creating new pages. Be careful, though, not to reproduce web page content without permission. For example, if you come across an essay that includes animated graphics of plant growth, you could borrow the HTML method for producing animated graphics, but you shouldn't use the images of plants used on that page unless you get permission from the person who created them or holds any copyrights to them.

Where to Find Netscape Navigator Copies and Information

Homepage
  http://home.Netscape.com/

Download page
  http://home.Netscape.com/comprod/mirror/index.html

Software FTP sites
  wuarchive.wustl.edu/packages/www/Netscape/netscape1.1/
  ftp.cps.cmich.edu/pub/Netscape/
  ftp.utdallas.edu/pub/Netscape/netscape1.1/
  ftp.micro.caltech.edu/pub/Netscape/
  unicron.unomaha.edu/pub/Netscape/netscape1.1/
  server.berkeley.edu/pub/Netscape/
  SunSITE.unc.edu/pub/packages/infosystems/WWW/clients/
    Netscape/
  magic.umeche.maine.edu/pub/Mirrors/nscape/consult.ocis.
  temple.edu/Big_Kahuna/Pub/Mac/Comm/ (Mac only)

10.3 Mosaic

Introduction

For more than a year, Mosaic ruled the Web. Appearing early in 1993, Mosaic was the first graphic browser to be widely adopted around the Net. It has been credited not only with capturing the imaginations of Net users from traditional domains (education, government, and military) but also with attracting the attention of the business community. In fact, it appeared for a while that Mosaic might follow such brand names as Kleenex and Xerox by becoming both a name for a specific product and a generic term. People were beginning to refer to "Mosaic" as both the browser and the Web itself.

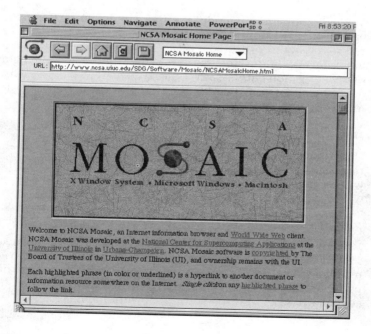

Marc Andreeson lead the team that created Mosaic at the National Center for Supercomputing Application (NCSA). In March 1994, Andreeson, along with several of his colleagues, left the center and began developing a commercial version of the browser, called Netscape, which quickly surpassed Mosaic as the most popular Web browser.

Still, Mosaic had a powerful effect on many people, especially on those who had previously been skeptical about the Web's range of possibilities. Stories of conversions from skeptic to believer are common: People would see the combination of voice, text, image, and color, the easy point-and-click graphic interface, how these features enhanced the hypertextual organization of the Web, and their eyes would pop.

Mosaic for Macintosh version 2.0b12 takes up about 2.2MB of disk space and runs best with 4MB of RAM.

Facts About Using Mosaic[1]

Navigation

Mosaic's hotlist resides under the Navigate menu in the menu bar. If you select Hotlist, Mosaic opens a dialog box that lets you add to the Hotlist or visit any pages listed there. The History feature is located in the "interface." It is the white box to the right of the navigation buttons. Select the box, and it will display a list of all the places visited during the current session. The Navigate menu also includes links to NCSA's homepages.

Default Page

Under the Options menu in the menu bar, you can choose "Use this page for home," and whatever page you are on at that time will become the default page. The next time you start Mosaic, it will load that page.

E-Mail

Mosaic's recent version allows you to send mail by following links created with the HTML Mailto tag, which means you can send e-mail if a web page developer includes e-mail access as part of the page. Unlike Netscape, you cannot generate original e-mail to anyone whose address you know from within Mosaic.

Netnews

Mosaic also allows you to read USENET newsgroups, but its interface is simpler than Netscape's.

---

1. These are based on the Macintosh beta version, 2.0b12.

View Source

The View Source feature can be found under the File menu in the menu bar.

Homepage

Here are the URLs for different versions of the Mosaic homepage. Each is slightly different and offers information specific to the Mosaic browser designed for each operating system listed.

All-purpose Mosaic homepage
   http://www.ncsa.uiuc.edu/SDG/Software/Mosaic/NCSA
      MosaicHome.html

MacMosaic homepage
   http://www.ncsa.uiuc.edu/SDG/Software/MacMosaic/Mac-
      MosaicHome.html

WindowsMosaic homepage
   http://www.ncsa.uiuc.edu/SDG/Software/WinMosaic/Home
      Page.html

XWindowsMosaic homepage
   http://www.ncsa.uiuc.edu/SDG/Software/XMosaic/

10.4 MacWeb and WinWeb

Introduction

TradeWave (formerly EINET) produces MacWeb (for Macintosh) and WinWeb (for PCs running MS Windows). These are very reliable graphic browsers for people with good access to the Net but using relatively low-end computers. Both programs do all the essential things graphic browsers do—display graphics, employ color, download sound and video files, and provide navigational aids for following the hypertextual documents on the Web. Since the MacWeb and the WinWeb interfaces are similar, we present only a screenshot of MacWeb at the top of page 106.

However, MacWeb and WinWeb sport few of the bells and whistles found in programs like Netscape and Mosaic. They do not handle the special HTML tags introduced by Netscape; in most cases, they simply ignore the HTML instructions they don't understand. For instance, if MacWeb encounters a page that includes the blinking effect produced by the "blink" tag, it will display the text as normal.

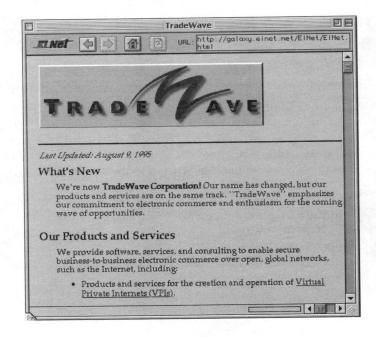

The main advanced HTML feature that causes problems for low-end browsers is tables. Browsers like Netscape and Mosaic, which have begun to incorporate features of the coming new standard for HTML (HTML 3), can produce tables that create rows and columns of information. When low-end browsers encounter tables, the information is often presented in some disarray. All the information is intact, but it can be difficult to read.

MacWeb and WinWeb each take up less than 500K of disk space and run best with 2MB of RAM though they can operate on as little as 750K (Mosaic's minimum is 2.7MB).

MacWeb and WinWeb Particulars

Navigation

The menu for recording favorite web pages is also called a Hotlist. Its History feature and its links to helpful sites are found under the Navigate menu in the menu bar.

E-Mail

These browsers do not support e-mail.

Netnews

MacWeb and WinWeb can read newsgroups, but like Mosaic, they provide a very simple interface.

View Source

View Source is found under the Options menu in the menu bar. The browsers offer several sub–options, but choose Retrieved in order to see the full HTML version of the page.

Homepage

Here are the URLs for different versions of the MacWeb or WinWeb homepages. Each homepage is slightly different and offers information specific to Macintosh or Windows browsers.

All-purpose MacWeb/WinWeb homepage
  http://galaxy.einet.Net/EINet/EINet.html
MacWeb homepage
  http://galaxy.einet.Net/EINet/MacWeb/MacWebHome.html
WinWeb homepage
  http://galaxy.einet.Net/EINet/WinWeb/WinWebHome.
    html

10.5 A Selection of URLs to Explore

http://WWW.w3.org/hypertext/WWW/History.html
  A timeline of the World Wide Web's development
http://WWW.w3.org/
  Homepage for W3, the World Wide Web Consortium, a collection of people and organizations working to continue the development of the Web
http://www.yahoo.com/Computers/Internet/World_Wide_
    Web/
  Yahoo's World Wide Web directory

CHAPTER 11

MOOs and MUDs

CHAPTER CONTENTS
  11.1 Introduction
  11.2 Telnet Help for MOOing

*People talk about cyberspace as if it were the future,
but cyberspace is here—this is it. People live online
in this world, and make friends here, and work here,
and play here.*

—Amy Bruckman, MediaMOO founder, on CNN, May 1993

11.1 Introduction

MOOs and MUDs are Internet software that allow users to meet online to converse, play games, hold classes and academic conferences, or—if a person registers as a member of a particular MOO or MUD—create a virtual room of one's own. MUD stands for Multi-User Dimension (or Dungeon since MUDs are often used for playing Dungeons and Dragons). MOO stands for

MUD, Object-Oriented. Object-oriented refers to a kind of pro-gramming language that lets programmers share bits of programs they write so that others can incorporate those bits into their own programs.

Because MOOs and MUDs are still associated with game play-ing and diversion, rather than work and academics, many schools do not allow students to access them during peak operating hours. Some ban them outright. However, more and more academic work is being done in MOOs and MUDs. They are being used for distance education classes, for cross-class collaboration, academic conferencing, and for learning foreign languages, to name only a few examples. Since most of our work occurs in MOOs, the fol-lowing examples and explanations will be from MOOs. However, most of the commands can be used in MUDs as well. In a MUD or MOO, whenever you are uncertain or confused, the command to remember is **help**. Type it and hit enter.

11.2 Telnet Help for MOOing

Since many schools do not offer support for using MOOs, most users' first experiences in MOOing is via Telnet.

Telnet, you may recall from Chapter 6, is an Internet tool that allows a person to connect to a remote computer. It allows the per-son's terminal to activate commands on the remote computer even though it may be on the other side of the world. Although that sounds exotic, it's really quite simple in concept. Connecting via Telnet is like making a phone call, only instead of dialing a number, you input an address.

To Telnet, you need to know the address you want to reach. Often you'll see addresses for MOOs given in "Telnet." Someone might write, "To get to SomeMOO, Telnet moo.somemoo.com 7777," which means to reach SomeMOO, you would type the fol-lowing at your Internet account prompt:

```
prompt%telnet moo.somemoo.com 7777
```

It is important not to put a space before typing telnet. Make sure you *do* put a space between the word *telnet* and the address, and a space between the final portion of the address name (in this case, .com) and the port number (in this case, 7777).

Viewing a MOO in Telnet

Telnet, though it will connect you to a MOO, is not a MOO client, such as TinyFugue or MUDDweller. It is a generic Internet tool designed for connecting to a remote computer. Therefore, when you Telnet to a MOO, there is no separate window or line for writing a message, then sending it; there is no automatic word wrap on the right margin, and the text does not automatically stop scrolling by before you can read it. Telnet merely accesses the software. A MOO or MUD client manages the MOO/MUD so that you can control margins, scroll, and send messages with greater ease.

MOOs do have commands that let you correct for the scrolling and word wrap problems you'll get with a Telnet connection; however, they cannot provide a separate window for writing your message. The scroll and wrap commands are **@pagelength** and **@linelength**, respectively.

To use these, do the following:

1. Telnet to a MOO.
2. Connect to the MOO. The command for this will be **co guest**.
3. Once in the MOO, type (as an example) **@pagelength 22**.
4. Then type (as an example) **@linelength 75**.

(You can experiment with different numbers to see what reads best in your screen.) In some MOOs, this command automatically activates word wrap so that words don't break at odd places on the right margin. In other MOOs, you need to type the command for word wrapping. You'll know if you need it because the MOO will send you a message that says, "linelength now 75, word wrapping is off." Some MOOs loose their word wrapping when the line length is changed. If the MOO doesn't send you a message, but still looses automatic word wrap when the line length is changed, you'll be able to tell because some of the words at the right margin will break in the middle and carry over to the next line. The command to activate word wrapping is **@wrap on**.

Once you have set the line length and made sure the word wrap feature of the MOO is active, the right margin will take care of itself. However, to manage scrolling, you will need to signal the MOO when you're ready to read the next screen of messages.

When you use **@pagelength**, the MOO will stop text from scrolling after the designated number of lines have scrolled onto the screen. You will see a line at the end of the text that says:

****More***** (# of lines) @more:rest:flush to continue.

If you type **@more**, you will get the next 22-lines of text. You will keep getting screens of text in 22-line increments every time you type **@more**.

If you type **@rest**, the text that is waiting will scroll by without stopping, even if it is more than the 22 lines you set as your page length.

If you type **@flush**, the text that is in the queue waiting to be read by you will be erased, and you'll see the first new message in the discussion since you typed **@flush**.

The **@more** command comes in especially handy if you decide to read a MOO's newspaper or some of its help files. You will also find it useful when you are in a fast-moving discussion. As you take time to write a message—and in Telnet interfaces, messaging takes time because it is hard to see what you are writing—messages from others who are in the room talking with you will be backed up for you, allowing you to speak and hear (write and read) at your leisure.

Sending a Message in Telnet

This is an unwieldy task. In Telnet interfaces on MOOs, you don't have a separate place for writing a message; instead, you must write on the same screen—in the same space—from which the messages you are reading emerge. Thus as you are entering a message, incoming messages interrupt your flow of writing.

In a MOO, to send a message, you type the command **say** (or its shortcut ") and then the text of your message. So if you were to say hello to someone in the room, you might type "**hi there, how are you?** After you press the Enter key, the message will be sent. You would then see on your screen:

You say, "hi there, how are you?"

Here's how writing a message looks in Telnet when, as you are writing, others are speaking.

"I really wish there Zeus says, "The god's must be crazy" was a way to
Athena [to Zeus] "well yes, if they start by hiding in the mother and
    to write these castrating
their father." ages without so much hecticness.

On a split screen, with a separate window for writing, the same words would look like this:

Zeus says, "The god's must be crazy"
Athena [to Zeus]: well yes, if they start by hiding in the mother and
    castrating their father.

"I really wish there was a way to write these messages without so
    much hecticness.

This feature, more than any other, compels MOO regulars to find a client.

Alternatives to Telnet

Clients are the best alternatives to Telnet. Which client you use depends on how you are connected to the Internet. When you connect to the MOO of your choice, the third thing you should do, after you set page length and line length, is type **help client**. Or you can connect via anonymous FTP to ftp.math.okstate.edu, and go to the directory/pub/muds/clients. Once you are in this directory you have four directory choices: UnixClients, VMSClients, misc, and vt. When you choose a client, make sure to note the compression extensions (.z, for example). Many users need to set up their clients on their Internet accounts, the account they log into with their modems.

The following example shows how to do this with TinyFugue in the UNIX operating system. We've shown you how to FTP and how to get a program; this example shows you how to uncompress a program once it is on your account:

```
prompt%ls
Mail     News      hold      tf.32b1.tar.gz tf.README
```

```
prompt%pico tf.README
```

Pico is the UNIX editor used to read the tf.README file that
was stored at the FTP server with the program. You'll notice the
use of all capitals in the filename to get your attention. Always
make sure to get any readme files associated with the software you
get through FTP. This readme file contained the following important information as part of its message:

```
gunzip tf.<version>.tar.gz   ;# or:  uncompress tf.<version>.tar.Z
tar -xof tf.<version>.tar
cd tf.<version>
more README
make
```

These are the steps to follow for decompressing the software.
Note the first line offers two different possibilities. Not all UNIX
servers will have the gunzip software, so the programmer of
TinyFugue has another version at the FTP site that a user can
choose instead. Learn what decompression software your Internet
server supports. In our example we use a UNIX account with gunzip. Thus to follow the directions to uncompress the file, type the
following:

```
prompt% gunzip tf.32b1.tar.gz
```

After a few seconds, the prompt returns. As the example pro-
gresses, you'll see how each command in the list from the
tf.README file is activated, followed by the ls command to show
the results.

```
prompt%ls
Mail                News      hold  tf.32b1.tar   tf.README
```

```
prompt% tar -xof tf.32b1.tar
prompt%ls
Mail                hold      tf.32b1.tar
```

News   tf.32b1   tf.README

prompt% **cd tf.32b1**
prompt%**ls**
CHANGES   CREDITS   Makefile   src
COPYING   Config   README   tf.lib

You'll note the list differs from the previous example. **cd** means to change directory. The files above are in a directory called tf.32b1.

prompt% **pico README**

This file gave information about the software's writer, suggested $10.00 as a fee for using the software, and gave some tips on how to use the **make** command, which activates a script that automatically installs the program on the account.

prompt% **make**

This **make** command activated the installation of TinyFugue on the Internet account in our example. It took about five minutes to complete and install successfully. However, depending on how your school configures its system, this might not always be

HELPFUL HINT: Before you activate the make command, turn on your communication's software screen capture. This feature captures everything that scrolls across your screen and saves it to a file. If you have a problem installing the software, a file like this could be helpful to someone trying to help you. In fact, screen capture is a useful tool to turn on whenever you try something new; it lets you review your steps. If you are working from a school computer, make sure to put a disk in and to save the capture file to the disk so that *you* have it.

CHAPTER

A MOO Walkthrough (Telnet)

CHAPTER CONTENTS
12.1 Introduction
12.2 MOO Etiquette

12.1 Introduction

This is a sample session we put together from a composite of rooms we have at different MOOs. SomeMOO is an imaginary MOO with real rooms in it. We purposefully compiled this as a way to give you a sense of how you might move about a MOO and use certain help commands. In this section, we activate the help commands so that you can see here what you will see on your screen. We suggest that the best way to use this chapter is to have it open when you log into a MOO or MUD for the first time. In this section, you will also meet Munchkin, the standard MOO example character. Munchkin first appears when we show you the help say command.

To begin the walkthrough, we Telnet to our imaginary MOO.

```
prompt% telnet moo.somemoo.com 7777
Trying...
Connected to moo.somemoo.com.
Escape character is '^]'.
```

Once connected, the following menu typically greets the user:

```
Type:
COnnect [Name] [password]       connect as existing player
CReate [Name] [password]        create a temporary player (not all
                                MOOs have this)

COnnect Guest                   connect as a guest
@who or Who                     see who's here now
@quit or Quit                   quit SomeMOO
```

With a Telnet interface, there is no prompt. The commands are typed in the flush-left, bottom portion of the screen.

```
@who
No one logged in.
co guest
*** Created ***
Welcome Station
You are inside a MOO Highway rest stop. You can grab a map, grab
    a snack, read the newspaper, The SomeMOO Times, or exit
    through the door to the north.
Obvious exits: north to the SomeMOO bus stop (catch a ride to
    town), south to virtual rest rooms, east to maps and vending
    machines, west to the newstand.
You see a note, a friendly tour guide, and a lost mitten.
```

We will move through three rooms. The Electric Pen and The Writery are rooms Nick and Eric have built in DaedalusMOO, a MOO sponsored and maintained by The Daedalus Group, designers of networked writing software used in many classrooms. For teachers who use Daedalus software in their classrooms, this MOO is a place to bring students for online conferencing and class meetings or to arrange collaborative projects across classes. The third room, The TechnoRhetoricians Bar and Grill, belongs to Eric. Its home is at MediaMOO, a MOO used by media researchers. MediaMOO is not a MOO for classes or student meetings.

@join nickc
The Electric Pen
It's a bit cluttered, of course, and you can't help but notice the sprawled sheaf of papers on the floor that break the occasional fall of a floppy disk from the teetering stack on the table above. Next to that table, in front of the window, an espresso machine sits on top of a dorm-style refrigerator. Around the room, along the walls, sit a set of matching chairs, a couch, and end-tables, with a coffee table in the center marred by cat scratches on the legs. The window is open slightly, letting a cool breeze waft in. Obvious exits: tw to The Writery
You see Bookcase here.
nickc is here.

Whenever you first enter a room, you are given its description. In this example, nickc built himself a grander office than he had at the time as a teaching assistant, where he met students in a basement office cramped with steam pipes and broken file cabinets. The description might also include other players who are in the room. You can talk to any player who is in the same room as you. Since MOOs are multiuser, there can be, depending on the circumstances, quite a few users.

@pagelength 24
Page length is now 24.
@linelength 80
Line length is now 80. Word wrapping is off.
@wrap on
Word wrap is now on.

Remember the importance of these commands for telnetters.

The **help communication** command is an example of using the help menu. Under this command, you will see a number of other commands for communicating with fellow MOOers:

say (or ")	Talk to the other players in the room
whisper	Talk privately to someone in the same room
emote	Nonverbal communication with others in the same room
page	Shout to a person in another or the same room
gagging	Screen out noise generated by certain other players
news	Read the wizards' most recent set of general announcements
@gripe	End complaints to the wizards
@typo @bug @idea @suggest	
	Send complaints/ideas to the owner of the current room
whereis	Locate other players
@who	Find out who is currently logged in
mail	The MOO e-mail system
security	The facilities for detecting forged messages and eavesdropping

Each of these commands leads to more specific help. Some examples follow.

If you type **help say**, you'll see the following:

Says anything out loud so that everyone in the same room hears it. This is so commonly used that there's a special abbreviation for it, the double quote (").

Munchkin types this:	"This is a great MOO!
Munchkin sees this:	You say, "This is a great MOO!"
Others in the same room see this:	Munchkin says, "This is a great MOO!"

The help files for MOOs are pretty much the same from MOO to MOO for basic commands. MOO software is available on the Net and can be set up on any Internet server. After that, each

MOO wizard, the person in charge of maintaining the MOO, will make his or her own customizations, often with the help of other wizards and members of the MOO community. MOOs evolve over time.

We'll also show you the syntax and official MOO examples for emote and page since they are frequently used.

If you type **help emote**, you'll see the following:

Announces anything to everyone in the same room. This is commonly used to express various nonverbal forms of communication. The abbreviation for the emote command is the colon (:)

| Munchkin types this: | :wishes he were much taller... |
| Everyone in the same room sees this: | Munchkin wishes he were much much taller... |

If you type **help page**, you'll see the following:

Sends a message to a connected player, telling them your location and, optionally, text.

Type page [player] [text].

Munchkin types this:	Page Frebble with "Where are you?"
Frebble sees this:	You sense that Munchkin is looking for you in the Kitchen.
Then Frebble sees this:	"Where are you?"
Munchkin sees this:	Your message has been received.

The **look** command helps you get your bearings. It's helpful if you forget where exits are or who is in the room with you.

```
look
The Electric Pen
Long room description deleted here for brevity.
Obvious exits: tw to The Writery
You see Bookcase here.
nickc is here.
```

To move from room to room, follow the exits by typing the command given after the obvious exits listed. Simply typing **tw** will move you to another room called The Writery. This is the meeting room for the Online Writery in Daedalus MOO. Students at the University of Missouri can login and come here to meet a writing tutor online to discuss their writing.

> **tw**
> The Writery
> More of an aroma than a room. You're reminded of baking bread. Rich coffee brewing. Warmth. Safety. Comfort. Donut holes. Community. Fingers stuck together with glaze. But there's something else cooking here. Not bread, but . . . (type: read welcome) [Note: conversations here may be logged, but only for record-keeping purposes.]
> Obvious exits: east to TR Bar and Grill, tep to The Electric Pen
> Eric (idling away--back soon) and Nick (drowsing...feel free to wake) are here.

We'll travel again, this time to a bar. The actual location of TechnoRhetoricians' Bar and Grill is the MediaMOO.

> **east**
> The TechnoRhetoricians' Bar and Grill
> A slovenly, comfortable hovel where the patrons discuss the rhetorical implications of every little thing, including the shifting dunes of crumbs and peanut shells that ripple across the floor. No one here is daunted by triviality.
> Obvious exits: north to the panopticon, west to The Writery, east to MOOReligion Courtyard, down to The Cell, and up to CWTA Outpost
> You see MacXVI, Lou the Bartender, Pony, Isocrates, Derrida, tool box, and Barthes here. MC, sm, Glenn, Eric [GPC], and beckster are here.

These represent the basic commands. The final command you need to know is how to leave a MOO, which is @quit.

@quit
Connection closed by foreign host.

12.2 MOO Etiquette

1. The first time you visit any MOO, you will login as a guest. Almost every MOO will have a welcome message for guests. In the message, there will often be directions for how to read the MOO's policies and guidelines for behavior. For example, the welcome message might advise you to read the acceptable use policy by typing **read aup**. If for some reason the MOO does not give you a direction like this, the following suggestions should keep you a guest in good standing.

2. Many MOOs are educational sites. Classes may be meeting. Students from across the country may be collaborating on projects. Don't interrupt this work by barging into a room and asking if anyone wants to talk.

3. When you log into a MOO, the first room you land in is usually a common room. Very often the rooms immediately off it have useful information and are considered public spaces. If you see another player in one of these rooms, the polite thing to do is say hello.

4. As you explore a MOO, you will move from room to room. The process will feel as if you are wandering in a labyrinth. However, many MOOs have maps as navigational aids. The help map command will tell you if the MOO you are in has a map and how to use it.

5. If you plan to visit a particular MOO regularly, you should request a character. **Help character** or **help register** commands will tell you whom to send e-mail to in order to do that. Many MOOs include this information in their welcome message or acceptable use file.

6. Sometimes as you are exploring a MOO and using the navigational commands to move from room to room, you will inadvertently enter a room while the owner and, perhaps, another player are in it. If so, they will usually say hello. Say hello back,

and let them know that you are just exploring. They may or may not wish to talk at that time. They might be building an object or doing some work. Therefore, if you wish to talk, always ask first if now is a good time for them to chat. Never launch into a conversation in these circumstances.

7. When you are done exploring a MOO, always use the @quit command to leave. This helps the MOO run more efficiently.

CHAPTER 13

OWLs and Other Birds of the Net

CHAPTER CONTENTS
13.1 OWLs
13.2 WIOLEs
13.3 List of Sites

13.1 OWLs

OWLs are not virtual birds of prey swooping around the Internet looking for hapless technorodents. They are writing center services that have migrated to the Net. OWL is an acronym for Online Writing Lab, and more than a few of them have sprung up in the past year or so. They are sources of information and assistance for student writers.

With a few exceptions (such as Dakota State's OWL), online writing labs are being developed by people who run face-to-face writing centers. Unlike their place–bound predecessors, though, OWLs generally are available as resources for students from any-where on the Internet, another case where the Net is crossing tra-ditional boundaries. They will not, nor are they generally intend-ed to, replace traditional writing centers. But online writing ser-vices and resources do offer things that are not available (at least not as conveniently) from traditional writing centers.

OWLs come in all shapes and sizes. Some consist mainly of an e-mail address where tutors respond to inquiries or read and com-ment on drafts of papers. Others are elaborate combinations of web pages, Gopher directories, e-mail access, mailing lists, news-groups, and MOOs. What all seem to have in common is a pur-pose: to provide student writers with assistance they cannot find in most classes.

Some OWLs provide writing reference material on mechanics and grammar; organization and idea generation; online versions of common writers' aids like dictionaries, thesauri, and style guides; sample papers; and sometimes essays by tutors offering writing advice. Some OWLs provide access to tutors via e-mail or MOOs so that students can ask questions about writing or submit drafts of papers for review.

The information or assistance that remote students can expect from an OWL may vary dramatically from one service to another. Keep in mind that even though they exist on the Internet, these services are sometimes limited by local conditions. Most OWLs must give priority to serving students at their own institutions. Some, however, welcome people from anywhere. For example, Purdue University's OWL (one of the first and most popular) cur-rently focuses on offering information about writing based on the printed handouts developed by its writing lab. Once the informa-tion has been provided for Purdue students, the university incurs very little additional expense in making it available to anyone on the Internet. Many people from places around the world have taken advantage of that resource.

The University of Missouri's Online Writery (http://www.mis-souri.edu/~wleric/writery.html) offers "cybertutors," people who are paid to help whoever inquires. Although priority is given to the university's students, as it happens, cybertutors often end up talk-ing to as many nonuniversity people (some of whom are not even students) as they do local students. This is the main distinction between OWLs and most traditional writing centers, where limitations on who can use the service are usually enforced strictly.

13.2 WIOLEs

WIOLE, or Writing Intensive Online Learning Environment, is a cousin to the OWL and has many similar characteristics, including network access to writing tutors and information about writing. The fundamental purpose of WIOLEs is to facilitate written conversation online. Conversations may include helping students with papers, but the emphasis is more on electronic written conversation as a legitimate end itself rather than merely as a means of improving printed texts. The emphasis might be said to shift from developing texts to developing ideas. Both OWLs, which are prevalent and growing in number, and WIOLEs, which may

emerge as key elements in online writing education, are valuable resources for students exploring the Net. The University of Missouri's Online Writery is an example of a WIOLE. In addition to its OWL services and web pages, it includes two mailing lists, two local newsgroups, and a MOO, giving students several channels through which to converse—synchronously or asynchronously. Certainly, Internet Relay Chat (IRC) could also serve as a venue for synchronous, or real-time, conversation.

13.3 List of Sites

The URLs listed here point to OWLs and WIOLEs that you might want to visit. We recommend that you explore a number of them to find the ones that might best fit your needs and interests. Of course, this list is by no means comprehensive (and certainly will not be by the time this book is published). But because most of these sites include links to other similar services, visiting one generally gives access to all. It's a matter of following the links until you find what you need.

We have not listed OWLs that primarily consist of e-mail. Some of those services may not be prepared for large numbers of inquiries, whereas others invite anyone to seek help from them. The Purdue OWL web pages, however, include a page with OWL e-mail addresses. We recommend looking there for a current list.

The parenthetical notes indicate our impression of the site's current main focus. Some sites have plans to expand their services, but have not yet developed those new services. "Local information" indicates that the site mainly provides information online about the local face-to-face writing center. "Writing information" means the site provides access to writing guides and help files. "Conversation" means the site provides access to tutors who are available to discuss writing over the Net.

National Writing Centers Association List of Online Writing Labs and Centers
http://www2.colgate.edu/dlw/NWCAOWLS.html
(comprehensive and annotated lists of OWLs)

Bowling Green University
Gopher://Gopher.bgsu.edu:70/11/Departments/write
(writing information)

**The CyberspaceWriting Center Consultation Project
(WritingWorks)**
http://fur.rscc.cc.tn.us/cyberproject.html
(conversation)

Dakota State University
http://www.dsu.edu/departments/liberal/cola/OWL/
(conversation)

Purdue University
http://owl.trc.purdue.edu/
(writing information)

Rensselaer Polytechnic Institute
http://www.rpi.edu/dept/llc/writecenter/Web/home.html
(writing information)

Trinity College
http://www.trincoll.edu/writcent/aksmith.html
(writing information, conversation soon)

The University of Michigan-Ann Arbor
http://www.umich.edu/~nesta/OWL/owl.html
(writing information, conversation)

The University of Missouri-Columbia
http://www.missouri.edu/~wleric/writery.html
(conversation)

The University of Oregon
http://darkwing.uoregon.edu/~jcross/word.html
(writing information)

CHAPTER

How to Create Your Own Basic Web Page

CHAPTER CONTENTS
14.1   The Web Changes Everything
14.2   Permissions
14.3   Introduction to HTML
14.4   HTML Basics
14.5   Sample HTML Document
14.6   Basic UNIX Commands

In the world of bits, you can be small and global
at the same time.
–Nicholas Negroponte, Wired, *April 1995*

14.1   The Web Changes Everything

The Web opens up new possibilities that just do not exist in a print-dominated world. Much of the hype surrounds the multimedia capability of the Web, the ease with which it allows writers to employ sound and image along with words. That's important, of course, but print already allows the juxtaposition of word and image, and sound recording is an accessible technology. What the

Web does that is so radical is put control of those various media into the hands of anyone with access and allows them to create with the media in new ways. Word, sound, and image can interact on the Web in ways they cannot with other technologies.

The publishing playing field is dramatically leveled, and the tools available to students and other writers are nearly as sophisticated as those available to large organizations and companies. The Web does not, by itself, democratize publishing, but it creates the conditions in which democratization is more likely to occur. Much of the information on the Web now, even on some of the "coolest" web pages, was put there not by professional writers and designers and scholars, but by whoever wanted to put it there. English students may view the Web not only as a place to find information but also as a place to put information. By adding their own work and ideas to the growing body of knowledge on the Net, writing starts to have a whole new meaning.

Creating web pages is not difficult. The learning curve for HyperText Markup Language is steep for about five minutes, then things level out and you're on your way. In fact, the learning curve is lessening. There are many programs available on the Net called HTML editors—many of them freeware or shareware—and some of them are getting very sophisticated. The most sophisticated and easy to use at the moment is PageMill, a commercial product by Adobe (http://www.adobe.com/Apps/PageMill/). PageMill is a WYSIWYG (What You See Is What You Get) program, so in that respect it is similar to the word processing programs you are probably familiar with. The need to learn HTML tags, or the commands browsers respond to, may become unnecessary as PageMill and other programs like it become more common. In the meantime, though, it is worth learning some HTML. And some would argue that it will be worth knowing HTML even after it is not absolutely necessary. Knowing the underlying structure of anything can have its advantages, especially when problems occur. Someone who knows what is going on behind the scenes is often better prepared to discover solutions.

Most web servers run on UNIX workstations (though there are versions for many other operating systems as well). UNIX is a computer operating system that comes in a number of different versions, but most have some basic commands in common. In addition to learning HTML, you will need to know some of those UNIX commands in order to create directories and files that can be read by your web server. Specific procedures for creating web directories and for uploading and downloading files may vary from place to place, but the HTML code within each web document will be common to everyone.

14.2 Permissions

The first thing to do, in most cases, is create a directory named www in your UNIX account. The UNIX command is **mkdir www**, and it is entered at the system prompt.

For files to be visible to web users, the permissions have to be set correctly. "Permissions" refers to determining who has the ability to read a file, make changes to it, or execute it (executable files, usually programs, are files that do something when launched). The files that will make up your web pages should be set so that you have permission to read and write, the group has permission to read, and all others have permission to read. Because your web directory should also be set so that it is executable, it requires a slightly different command modifier.

To change files and directories, use the command chmod. For example, if I create a file called html_sample.html, I would need to set the permissions by typing at the system prompt **chmod 644 html_sample.html**. If I redisplay the directory (by typing **ls -al**), I should see in the file's permissions area:

-rw-r-- r--

The first hyphen (-) means this is a file, not a directory (if it were a directory, the string would read drw-r--r--). The following rw- refers to the permissions for you, the user. You can read the file and write new information in it. The first r-- refers to permissions for the group. Groups are defined groups of user IDs. For example, at the University of Missouri one group is all users with student accounts. Another group is users with faculty or staff accounts. In this case, anyone with a user ID in your group will be able to read the file but will not be able to make any changes to it. The second r-- refers to permissions for anyone else, including users who are not on your system. Again, anyone outside the group will be able to read the file but will not be able to write to it.

To correctly set the permissions on your web directory, type **chmod 755 www** when you are in your home directory. The result should look like this when you type **ls -al** (x indicates executable):

```
drwxr-xr-x
```

14.3 Introduction to HTML

Web documents are just text files, the kind that can be created with any word processor or text editor on just about any computer platform or operating system. What makes a text file a web document is the presence of HyperText Markup Language. To be more precise (since web browsers can also read plain text documents without HTML), HTML provides the means to create hypertext and hypermedia documents. HTML is what tells the web browser how to format the content of a file and where to take users who follow links.

Hypertext, by the way, refers to systems of organizing information associatively rather than sequentially. Books are fundamentally sequential in the way they organize information. They are designed to be read one page after another, one chapter after another, beginning to end. Hypertext allows you to jump from one place to another without following a preset sequence. That is, readers follow associations, or webs if you will, of meaning.

You are already familiar with a kind of hypertext if you've ever read a book that had an index. If you start at the beginning of the book, the table of contents maps out the sequence of information. If you start at the end, with the index, the order is alphabetical, and you choose specific bits of information based on the content you expect to find rather than by page sequence. You can leap around in the book if you use the index as your map. Hypertext software and systems like the Web mainly automate that "index" approach to reading.

HTML consists of a set of tags that provide instructions to web browsers viewing the document. Tags are simple codes enclosed in angle brackets (< >). There are instructions to the web browser telling it how to format the document or telling it how to find image files or documents at the other end of links. Most people are familiar with this process even though they don't often think about it. Consider a typical word processor. It has commands or menu choices that make text bold or italic, change the margins, increase font size, and so on. Each of these formatting features is controlled by tags, but in most word processors, the tags are invisible. They are embedded in the document so that the program can display text correctly, but out of the way of users as they create the document. With HTML, writers have to deal with the tags directly.

14.4 HTML Basics

All HTML files should end with .html or .htm following the filename. For example, the homepage for *RhetNet, A Cyberjournal for Rhetoric and Writing*, is rhetnet.html. Many HTML tags come in pairs, one to begin a formatting command and one to end the command. One of the most common errors new HTML writers make (the authors included) is to leave out an ending tag or fail to include the slash mark that differentiates the ending tag from the beginning tag.

Tags must be enclosed in angle brackets. For example, each document should begin with an <HTML> tag designating it as an HTML document. The ending tag, which in this case goes at the end of the document, is </HTML>.

Documents have two main parts, the head (<HEAD></HEAD>) and the body (<BODY></BODY>), which serve as containers for the contents of the file. The head element often contains only the document title tag though other special items can be used there.

The <TITLE></TITLE> tag holds the title of the window in which the document is displayed, so the text in the title tag will appear in the title bar of the browser window, not in the document itself. For that reason, titles are often short versions of the document's main heading.

Here's an example of the beginning of a typical HTML document:

```
<HTML>
<HEAD>
<TITLE>Sample HTML Document</TITLE>
</HEAD>
```

The body element contains all the things you see in the web page when it is displayed by a browser. The most common HTML features used in web pages are headings, paragraphs, lists, links, and images. There are many other possibilities, but knowing how to do these will be enough to get started.

<H> Headings

The <H> tag always includes a number from 1 to 6. <H1></H1> creates the dominant presence on the page, <H2></H2> is a bit smaller, <H3></H3> smaller yet, and so on. Note that the <H> tags do not refer to a specific font and size. They describe the size of the characters relative to the plain text in the document. The actual size and font may vary depending on the default setting of the browser or on changes users have made to their own copy of the browsers. For example, <H1> might be 24-point Palatino on my copy of Netscape, but it might be 20-point Geneva on MacWeb (or on someone else's copy of Netscape, for that matter).

<P> Paragraphs

The paragraph tag has long been one of the exceptions to the rule that tags come in pairs. <P> by itself is currently sufficient to separate paragraphs (<P> literally invokes a hard return followed by a line space). In the next version of HTML, however, the paragraph tag will become a pair, <P></P>, so it may be a good idea to get in the habit of starting paragraphs with <P> and ending them with </P>.

<L> Lists

There are several kinds of lists in HTML, but the most common are unordered list, <UL></UL>, ordered list, <OL></OL>, and definition list, <DL></DL>. In the case of ordered and unordered lists, the items in the list are preceded by <LI>, which is another tag that does not require a closing tag. Definition lists include two elements, the term to be defined, <DT>, and the definition itself, <DD>.

<A HREF> Links

This is the tag (Hypertext REFerence) that links words or images into links to other places in the file or to other places on the Web. What falls between <A HREF> and </A> is the address of the destination for users following the link. There are shortcuts, but here we will include only the full version of the tag. The address should be a URL, so include the server address, the directory path, and the filename of the destination.

<IMG SRC> Image Source

Several common image file formats are in use on the Web. These different formats are roughly analogous to the difference in format between documents created in different word processing programs, between Microsoft Word and WordPerfect, for instance. The most common and easiest-to-use image format is GIF. Others, especially JPEG, will work fine, but when you get started, you might want to convert any images you use to GIF format and make sure the filename ends with .gif. Not all graphics programs include GIF and JPEG as formats you can save files in, so if you get into web publishing much, you may want to find a conversion utility program, like GIFConverter, for the Macintosh. GIFConverter is a shareware program that converts standard formats like TIFF and PICT into GIF or JPEG (see http:// www.kamit.com/gifconverter.html). This all looks like alphabet soup now, but these acronyms will become part of your vocabulary quickly if you do much web publishing, even if you do not know what they stand for.

The main reason to use GIF is that all graphic browsers can include GIF images inline, which means the images appear right in the window with the text. Netscape will do that with JPEG images, but many other graphic browsers still require a helper application to display a JPEG image, so the image appears in a new window. For example, the logo for the Conference on College Composition and Communication, which appears on the organization's convention homepage (see http://www.missouri.edu/ ~cccc96/), has a filename of CCC.gif.

You don't have to possess image files in order to use them on your page, you just need to know the URL for their location on the

Web. To find that, you can use the View source command on graphic browsers to see the address in the <IMG SRC> tag of the image you want to use. It is very common to borrow HTML coding and image files from others on the Web. Be advised, though, that web authors may have copyright to some images, so it is safer and more courteous to write to a page author and ask for permission to use any image.

14.5 Sample HTML Document

You can use the following document as a template. Replace the text between the tags with your own information, put this document in a www directory on a machine with a web server, change the permissions, and you will have a web page of your own.

```
<HTML>
<HEAD>
<TITLE>Sample HTML</TITLE>
</HEAD>
<BODY>
<H1>This is a sample HTML page</H1>
<H2>This is a subhead sample</H2>
<P>

This is just a regular paragraph. Kind of boring.</P>

<P>

This is a second paragraph. It's not much more interesting than the first one.</P>

<P>
```

To spice things up a bit, we'll put a link to another site, to <A HREF=http://www.missouri.edu/~wleric/writery.html>The Online Writery</A>, an online writing and learning environment based at the University of Missouri. If you look at this document on the Web, the words "The Online Writery" will appear highlighted in some way, often with the color blue and underlining.</P>

<UL>
<LI>This is an unordered list
<LI>Most browsers will interpret the "LI" tag as a bullet
<LI>You can make this list as long or short as you like
<LI>I've run out of items to put here, so I'm going to close this list
</UL>

<OL>
<LI>This is an ordered list
<LI>The main difference from the unordered list
<LI>Is that the "LI" tags are displayed as numbers: 1, 2, 3, etc.
</OL>

<DL>
<DT>Definition list
<DD>A definition list is a list that displays the term at the left margin and the definition about five spaces to the right.
<DT>This is another link to the <A
HREF=http://www.missouri.edu/~wleric/writery.html>Writery
</A> is an example of a homepage using a definition list.
<DT>Another term
<DD>Another, much less interesting, definition
</DL>

<P>

Here are two simple .gif files. Both are simple arrows that we drew using HyperCard. They aren't very pretty, but you're welcome to use them if you like.
</P>

<IMG SRC="http://www.missouri.edu/~wleric/rtarrow.gif">
<IMG SRC="http://www.missouri.edu/~wleric/lftarrow.gif">

</BODY>
</HTML>

To see what this page looks like on the Web, access your local web browser and type in the following URL: **http://www.marlboro. edu/~nickc/vrpr/ericsamp.html.**

14.6 Basic UNIX Commands

As you can see by now from our combined FTP examples from Chapters 8 and 9, as well as the recent examples for writing your own web pages, knowing a little bit of UNIX helps a great deal when moving about on the Internet. You won't need this often, but we include these basic commands here for when you do.

Remember that UNIX is case sensitive. A file called send-money.txt is different from Sendmoney.txt. For this reason, if you name files when saving to a UNIX system, choose names that are long enough to let you know what is in the file, but also short enough to minimize the chance of error in managing the file. UNIX allows filenames to be up to thirty characters long. Using eight or so characters plus a three-character extension (similar to DOS for PCs) should be a workable length.

HELPFUL HINT: When saving software files to a UNIX account before downloading it to your own computer, it is best not to change the name or extensions of the file. Often a software file may have more than one extension, for example, untaranduncompress.sit.hqx. We recommended saving it that way so that when it is downloaded to your computer, you know exactly what software you will need to decompress it. In this case, StuffIt Expander would decompress the BinHex (.hqx) first, and the StuffIt (.sit) next, with one command. To avoid errors in downloading, you can use a wildcard in UNIX. Thus, if you were using zmodem protocol to download the file, you could type **sz untar*** at your prompt. This will download any file beginning with the name untar.

Basic UNIX Commands

ls	Lists files and subdirectories in your current directory.
ls -l	Lists files and subdirectories, shows their size, last date they were modified, and the user rights assigned to them.
ls -la	Lists everything indicated with ls -la, as well as files and subdirectories beginning with a period. For example, if you use Gopher, your UNIX account will have a file called .gopherc, a configuration file that tells Gopher what your preferences are. Most files and directories that begin with a period are for working in the background with programs.
cd	Changes a directory.
cdup	Used in FTP servers to move back one directory.
cd ..	Used in UNIX accounts to move back one directory (note the space between cd and ..).
chmod	Changes the modification or user rights for files and directories. chmod works by "totaling" the array of rights you wish to assign to a file. In making the file example.htm available for use on the Web, for example, you would type **chmod 644 example.htm**. That would make the file a combination of modes: 400 + 200 + 40 + 4. The owner of the file can read it and write in it; a group and other users can only read it. Here are the chmod commands you are most likely to use in UNIX:
400	read by owner
200	write by owner
100	execute, or search if file is a directory, by owner
40	read by group
20	write by group
10	execute, or search if file is a directory, by group
4	read by others
2	write by others
1	execute, or search if file is a directory, by others
cp	Copies a file. To copy test.txt to testback.txt, you would type **cp test.txt testback.txt**.
mkdir	Makes a directory. To create a directory called hold, you would type **mkdir hold**. You can then type **cd hold** to go into it.

mv   Renames a file. To change the name of the file called test3.txt to testpass, you would type **mv test3.txt testpass**.

pwd   Shows you which directory you are in.

rm   Removes files. Be careful not to type *, which is a UNIX wildcard. The command **rm *** will remove all files in a directory, including files that are essential to logging in and operating software if they are in that directory. If you want to remove a number of files, but not all, the command **rm -i*** will prompt you for a yes or no before each file, allowing you to work through the directory quickly. Be careful not to type **y** when you mean **n**.

rmdir   Removes a directory. To remove the directory called hold, you would type **rmdir hold**. A directory must be empty of files before it can be removed.

PART
three

RESEARCH

Chapter 15. Plagiarism, Copyright, and the
            Internet
Chapter 16. Citing Computer Programs and
            Electronic Documents

CHAPTER 15

Plagiarism, Copyright, and the Internet

CHAPTER CONTENTS
15.1 Introduction
15.2 The Difference Between Paper and Pixels
15.3 Three Serious Concerns
15.4 Concern One: Honesty
15.5 Concern Two: Stability and New Forms of Scholarship
15.6 Concern Three: Plagiarism Meets Copyright

Thomas Jefferson never considered that every citizen could enter every library and borrow every book simultaneously, with a key stroke, not a hike.
—Nicholas Negroponte, Wired, January 1995

In the absence of the old containers, almost everything we think we know about intellectual property is wrong. We're going to have to unlearn it. We're going to have to look at information as though we'd never seen the stuff before.
—John Perry Barlow, Wired, March 1994

15.1 Introduction

Teachers, as you know, are concerned about plagiarism. It is viewed as one of the worst academic sins anyone can commit. Every English handbook includes a chapter on citing sources, on how to avoid plagiarism by knowing the difference between paraphrasing, summarizing, and quoting. Every student handbook we've seen details the academic penalties for plagiarism. Most introductory college writing courses require students to write a term paper, and to use and document outside sources. Many such courses include a tour of the school library to get an overview of how to use its resources.

In this section of the book, we offer an overview of the Internet that invites you to think of it as an *electronic library* where you can find and use a seemingly inexhaustible array of resources. As you read through this section, keep in mind your school's or English teacher's definition of plagiarism and the standards that your institution has adopted. Even if you haven't learned them yet, dig out your student handbook or English handbook and review it. You want to keep those standards in mind as you conduct research on the Internet.

15.2 The Difference Between Paper and Pixels

Libraries have been part of academic culture for thousands of years. Our culture reveres the printed word. In Washington, D.C. the Library of Congress attempts to catalog and store every book published in the United States. As students, you learn to turn to books for knowledge; you are taught how to take notes from them, how to study them, and how to recall and use what you have read in them. The importance of books is in part tied to their permanence. Once a book is printed and bound, it can be used again and again. This ability for a book to circulate, to be read more than once, is what makes libraries and scholarship possible.

One reason academia places so much emphasis on citing a source correctly is so that when someone reads the essay in which a source is cited, he or she can use the citation to go to a library and get the exact book or article the author cited. Perhaps you have done research this way already, by using the bibliography of one book or article as a way to find more information on a subject. This tool of scholarship works so well because the researcher is confident that he or she will be able to read the same work, in the same form (or edition in bibliographical terms), that the author did. Reading an article in full allows the scholar to better judge it. He or she can see, for example, if the author used the source fairly and did not take any part of it out of context. The beauty of print is that it is fixed and therefore fairly reliable.

The Internet is not a print library. It comes to you in pixels. Pixels are the individual dots on your computer screen that combine to form letters, words, and images. Unlike print, pixels are very fluid. They can be changed, moved, deleted, and copied with a few keystrokes. This fluidity offers both exciting advantages and some serious concerns for researchers working on the Internet.

15.3 Three Serious Concerns

Unfortunately for students, plagiarism is an overextended term. It is used to describe a variety of flaws, from an unintentional error in paraphrasing a source to the sad practice of how some students will "borrow" another student's essay and pass it off as their own. The first is a natural mistake in the learning process, one that is inevitably going to occur in every classroom given the complexity of learning how to paraphrase correctly. The other is fraud, and sometimes even theft.

One concern we have heard is that students might be tempted by the ease with which an essay from the Internet can simply be copied and pasted, in part or in whole, into a student's file and then handed in as the work of the student. People are concerned students will be tempted to fraud and theft.

A second concern of researchers and teachers about sources found on the Internet is their stability. Will they be there tomorrow, and if they are, will they be the same version as they were the day before? The Internet is in constant flux. Sites close down, addresses change, people who put information online change or loose their access. Some sources of information are works in progress that undergo frequent revision and updating, or sources may simply be changed because a writer has changed his or her mind about what was in it. Some sources are new forms: archived e-mail discussions, logs of MOO meetings, collaborative hypertext essays. Do these deserve the same stature as a rigorously written article appearing in a highly regarded academic journal?

A third concern, one for writers who put their work online to consider, is the difference between plagiarism and copyright violation. A student may hand in a paper that analyzes a poem he or she read in *The New Yorker* magazine. In so doing, the student might very well include the full text of the poem and would no doubt cite it correctly, giving full credit and bibliographical infomation about the poem. He or she will easily satisfy all the rules for academic citing and will not have committed plagiarism. In the traditional classroom where a paper is read only by fellow students and a teacher, the inclusion of the full text of the poem is not a problem. However, if the student puts the essay on the Internet, perhaps as part of a collection of class essays, the poem will in effect be published. It will be available to anyone on the Internet—millions of potential readers. *The New Yorker* and the poet face a possibility of lost revenues because a poem they are trying to sell is now available for nothing. Thus, in this example, though the use of the poem would not be plagiarism, it would be a copyright violation.

15.4 Concern One: Honesty

Teachers and students both should be concerned about the fraud and theft of another writer's words. It is wrong to pass off the work of another as one's own, no matter what technology is used to complete the crime. Before digital technology and electronic files, students and established authors simply rewrote or retyped the already printed words of others with whatever writing technology was at hand: quill, pen, or typewriter. (Yes, students are not the only people to steal ideas and words. See Thomas Mallon's excellent history and overview of plagiarism, *Stolen Words: Forays into the Origins and Ravages of Plagiarism*, New York: Ticknor and Fields, 1989.) People who decide to cheat and steal will not be stopped by returning to an older technology. Technology does not determine integrity.

Consider the Complexities of Collaboration

Although it is wrong to steal, keep in mind that the Internet can encourage both planned collaboration and learning and thinking by osmosis. When collaboration is planned, students and teachers can arrange ways to keep track of who does what and how to evaluate it. However, some collaboration occurs just from bringing people together. Consider, for example, that in e-mail discussions it is not unusual to absorb an idea into one's own writing and thinking. A student may pick up on an idea mentioned in a message and expand on it in her own message; she may be asked a question about her expansion that makes her rethink and refine it. After her refinement, another writer might add a new twist to the idea. The student might take the new twist and add it to her evolving sense of the idea. She might save a copy of the message that sums up her final position and download it to use in an essay. That downloaded message represents the work of three or four people; the student acted as a synthesizer and editor (as did the others in the discussion), borrowing ideas and reshaping them in light of new ideas.

To our minds, and this is what we recommend to our students, the student in this scenario would not be plagiarizing if she used any of her messages, including the downloaded one summing up her final position, a position obviously influenced by other writers. The ideas in question, even the words in question, cease to be the intellectual property of this or that writer. In the give and take of the discussion, as words are shared and merged, participating earns the writer the right to the words that emerge. However, keep in mind that if the student downloads another author's e-mail message, she must cite that.

Keep a Writing Portfolio and Research Log

Many teachers wisely advise students to save all the writing they do while drafting an essay, everything from first notes and brainstorming ideas, to drafts, to feedback notes from those who read the essay for you. Some teachers will ask you to keep journals to reflect on your writing or to keep track of your research. If you decide to use the Internet for research, using these ideas—keeping drafts and making reflective writing and reading journal entries—will show that any essay you hand in has evolved from your own work.

Use Mixed Fonts

Another way to address concerns about the malleability of electronic sources is to make sure you do not mix a source's words into your own in the drafting process. Use the computer to help you see what words are yours and what words are a source's by using different fonts. For example, you might write your words in `courier 12 point font`, and save the text from any of your download sources in a font that is starkly different, say, perhaps **helvetica 14 point bold font.**

> HELPFUL HINT: Earlier we mentioned the complexity of paraphrasing. If you consult an English writing handbook, you'll see that the key to paraphrasing is accurately mixing your words with another author's. This means you have to be diligent about where you place quotation marks and footnotes or references. By using for your text a font different from that used for your source's text, you'll give yourself a visual aid when paraphrasing. As part of your final draft proofreading, simply put quotes around the paraphrased text. And don't forget to convert all fonts to the same font when your documentation and quotation marks are in place.

15.5 Concern Two: Stability and New Forms of Scholarship

Stability is a harder concern to address because so much of the Internet is not stable. However, there are safeguards a researcher can use to help assure that those who read his or her work will be able to find the sources cited.

Brand Names

One safeguard is to look for sources that come with a brand name. For example, *Time Magazine* maintains a presence on the

Internet (http://www.timeinc.com). If an English student were writing an essay on Jane Austen's *Sense and Sensibility*, and wanted to refer to how movie reviewers commented on the difference between the novel and the film, using the *Time* web page to access a review would not be a problem because Time Inc. has made a commitment to being online. Of course, there's no way of telling which publishers will stay on the Internet, but generally speaking, brand names are a useful indicator of permanence. Brand names do not mean, by the way, only commercial enterprises. Different academic groups maintain constant Internet presences, and often they are sponsored or affiliated with a college or university. Thus, for example, sources found on Carnegie Mellon University's English Server, (http://english-server.hss.cmu.edu/),which are vast and eclectic, are likely to be relatively stable.

Institutional Addresses

By institutional address, we mean the address of any company, educational institution, governmental agency, or group able to maintain their own Internet servers. You can usually tell this by their address. For example, Houghton Mifflin's web address is http://www.hmco.com/, hmco being the initials for Houghton Mifflin Company; this kind of address tells you that the source has direct control over the server. Such an address is not a guarantee of the site being stable, nor we imagine, that the source named in the address controls the server. But it usually indicates a significant commitment to an Internet presence and thus increases the chance that those who follow in the trail blazed by your works cited page will find the same path.

Personal Addresses

Look to see if an address includes a ~ with a name. For example, addresses for Nick's pages at Marlboro College all begin http://www.marlboro.edu/~nickc/. An address such as this means that the person whose name appears after the ~ is affiliated with the institution that runs the server indicated in the beginning of the address. These types of addresses will, as a general rule, be more temporary and subject to change than ones with paths directly to institutionally sponsored information.

Yes, but What About Stability?

You'll notice all the qualifiers in the paragraphs preceding this one: "as a *general* rule," "increases the *chance*," "*usually* indicates." We couldn't exactly give you a stable answer. Simply put, there is no stability. Not yet. Perhaps not for a long time, at least not any kind of stability that print enjoys. Print and publishing is an industry; there are financial interests (in academe, authors are paid with appointment, promotion, and tenure; thus the phrase *publish or perish*) that have helped solidify, over time, procedures for citing and documenting printed sources. Print sources also are stable. Journals and magazines and publishers come and go, but once something is printed, it is fixed; if it is reprinted, it is given a new edition number, or an editor will include a note telling you where it had been printed before. Print is fixed; pixels are fluid. That won't change.

Eventually, scholars will adjust to the fluidity of the Internet, and those who write online regularly will learn methods for saving their work and marking updates and additions. In fact, the Online Computer Library Center (OCLC, go to http://ora.rsch.oclc.org/oclc/menu/t-home1.htm) is working out ways to catalog Internet resources so that when you use an OCLC computer in your campus library to view its catalog of books, you'll be able to also get Internet references. In the meantime, when you question if a source will be there for another scholar to use, save the work on a diskette. If someone reads what you wrote and can't connect to the source you cited, he or she can always contact you, and you can e-mail the person a copy of what you used.

Journals and Peer Review

When searching for an online academic journal to use in your research, one aspect important to many scholars is whether the journal is peer reviewed. In peer reviewed journals, an author submits an essay for consideration. The journal's editor sends copies of the essay to other scholars in the same field as the essay's subject addresses. These scholars read the essay to make sure its research is up to date and accurate, to see if it is well written and properly documented, and to judge whether it is timely and offers ideas of value to the scholarly community it addresses. For this reason, journals that are peer reviewed are usually regarded as worthy sources (both on the Internet and in print). However, as useful as peer review is (it's helped enormously with this book), scholars are using new ways to build knowledge.

New Kinds of Academic Excellence

A good researcher should not limit himself or herself to just those sources that have a brand name, academic affiliation, or peer review publication procedure. For example, many journals are experimenting with nonpeer reviewed submissions. Others are making use of genres available only on the Internet: symposia carried out by e-mail, MOOs used to do presentations for academic conferences, or collaborative essays and hyperfiction. These new forms for scholarship are radically different from the traditional vehicle of the published-in-print paper or book. Instead of reading an article by a sole author, the Internet may present you with a multisided perspective on an issue.

15.6 Concern Three: Plagiarism Meets Copyright

Digital technology is premised on copying. Every time you call up a file to your screen, you are calling up a copy of the original file as it resides on someone's computer. If you send a friend the file, you are not sending him or her your copy of the file, you are sending him or her a copy of your copy of the file. This ability to copy work—whether the file is digitized words, music, graphics, or moving pictures—has led many people and organizations to call for restrictions on sharing electronic information. Right now there is a controversy on how to balance the rights of authors and publishers to protect their work versus the rights of others to access and duplicate it.

For now, however, we'd like to turn to a more immediate practicality. If you do place an essay on the Internet, you could be subject to and held accountable for copyright provisions as described in the scenario where a student writes an analysis of a *New Yorker* poem. Although the chances of a student's class assignment attracting much attention on the Internet is low, considering all the information out there, students and teachers who work online should follow the same guidelines on copyright that publishers use.

Material in the public domain may be quoted freely. Many electronic text archives, such as those maintained by Project Gutenberg (http://jg.cso.uiuc.edu/PG/welcome.html), are composed of works in the public domain. Authors hold a copyright on their work for their lifetime. Their heirs or publishers can keep the copyright for another fifty years. Fifty years after the death of the author, the material is considered to be in the public domain.

For quoting from copyrighted works, use the following rules of thumb:

1. You can quote excerpts of 300 words from a book or 150 words from a magazine or newspaper article if the following conditions are met:

   The excerpt is not a complete unit in the larger work from which you found it, such as a poem in a magazine, a chapter in a book, an article in a newspaper, or a list of rules in a manual.

   The excerpt makes up less than 20 percent of the total words in your source document.

   The excerpted words are integrated into your essay and do not stand alone as an anthology or chapter opening.

   You give full credit to the author, source, and publisher.

2. If you quote several short quotations from a source, and the total more than 300 words for a book or 150 words for a magazine or newspaper, you must get permission to use the quote.

3. You should get permission for using e-mail messages, including those you find in USENET, and unpublished writing such as personal letters sent to you, diary entries, and classmates' essays. Because poems are usually smaller units within larger works, you should get permission for more than four lines or 20 percent of the poem, whichever comes first.

These are the publishing industry's current standards for judging fair use and getting copyright permissions. They are offered only as a guideline and do not, of course, represent a legal definition or legal advice. Each book you use will indicate who holds the copyright on the work in the book. You will usually find that information on the title page. If a book quotes another work, you might also see a separate acknowledgment on the copyrights page; these acknowledgments will give you names you can look up to get addresses on. You can write to copyright holders to request permission. It is best when doing so to let the copyright holder know why you are writing, how you plan to use the copyrighted work, and where it will be appearing online. For example, if you hand in a class essay, it might be online for only one semester. If you submit a poetry review to an online literary magazine, it could be there indefinitely. These differences may be important to the copyright holder.

If you decide to quote lengthy excerpts from works you find online, they will often include an e-mail address that belongs to the copyright holder; this makes it easy to write for permission. E-mail is an example of copyrighted work (it is automatically copyrighted) for which you need permission; other essays you find online should be checked for permission. One advantage to using online sources, especially if you are working in the Web, is that you can easily include a link to the source. Many people who contribute online work will place a message in their work that declares the extent and type of copyright they hope to enforce. A common one reads, "This work may be redistributed freely, in whole or in part, but cannot be sold or used for profit or as part of a product or service that is sold for profit."

Remember, you need permission only to quote the copyrighted *words* of others. We will not get into the sticky subject of using copyrighted images and music. Just keep in mind that ideas cannot be copyrighted; only the expression (the particular arrangement of words) an author uses can be copyrighted. Thus you can summarize and restate any work in your own words. However, as you know from referring to an English handbook, when you do summarize, you must still cite the source so that you do not commit plagiarism.

CHAPTER 16

Citing Computer Programs and Electronic Documents

CHAPTER CONTENTS
16.1 Tips on Creating Correct Citations
16.2 Working with Files Accessed from the Internet
16.3 Citation Guidelines
16.4 Modern Language Association (MLA) Style Guidelines
16.5 American Psychological Association (APA) Style Guidelines
16.6 *The Chicago Manual of Style* (CMS) Guidelines

16.1 Tips on Creating Correct Citations

Remember, electronic sources are growing faster than scholars can find conventions for citing them, so you might easily find a source for which no one has offered a sample entry. Therefore, keep the following tips in mind.

Be Consistent with Other Citations

If you can't find an example for the source from what's in this guide, use your best judgment, and try to be consistent. The punctuation you use to separate the elements of your citation (author's name, document title, source, date, and so on) should be consistent with the punctuation used in other citations. Also make sure the order of elements is as consistent as possible with your other citations.

Don't Be Afraid to Give Too Much Information

Remember you are citing both to credit your source and to allow interested readers the information they will need to find the source for themselves. It is better to err in providing too much information than not enough.

Consider Using Explanatory Footnotes When Needed

Since you are working with new media, you might need to include explanatory footnotes about the sources. For example, here's an explanatory footnote used in an essay written about grading papers. The authors know that not everyone reading their essay will be familiar with an e-mail discussion list called Megabyte University (MBU).[1]

16.2 Working with Files Accessed from the Internet

Keep Careful Records

The Internet is teeming with online text, video and audio clips, graphic arts of all kinds, computer software, and other resources.

---

1. "Megabyte University" (MBU) is an Internet-based listserv (an electronic discussion group) that focuses on issues of computers and the teaching of writing. Colleagues interested in this discussion subscribe to the list and receive any messages sent to the list by any other list member. MBU was founded by Fred Kemp of Texas Tech. University. You can join via e-mail by leaving the subject line blank and sending the message **subscribe mbu-l yourfirstname yourlastname** to **listproc@listserv.ttu.edu**.

Nearly none of it is cataloged with any of the precision you would find in a library. Therefore, for everything you access, you must take special care to record in your notes what Internet tool you used to find it, as well as the name of the file as it appears online. Unlike a library source, if you don't write this information down the first time you find the source, you may not be able to remember how you found it later. If the computer you use allows you to copy and paste among different windows and programs, keep a file handy (on a diskette if the computer is not yours) for Internet addresses.

Note Version Numbers

Be aware of such things as version numbers and dates. Note that there may be two dates: the date it was originally put online and the date you read it. Many of the sources on the Internet are subject to change by the authors who wrote them. Make sure you note the version number and date of what you use so that your readers will know if they've accessed an incarnation different from what you read.

Remember That Pagination Will Vary

Different online journals use different conventions for measuring length. You know printed articles use page numbers, but online there are no page numbers as you normally conceive of them— there's no paper. Some articles will number paragraphs. Others will place markers in the article, looking something like

---#---

to indicate where a page ends. Still other journals or documents will have no discernible page marking or paragraph numbering system. Depending on what Internet tool you use to access the document, you may see a page indicator on your screen.

If you look at this screen snapshot of The Magna Carta, you see in the upper right-hand corner the notation, "Magna Carta, 1215 (p1 of 27)." In this particular interface—Lynx running on a UNIX server that was reached by a modem from a Macintosh using Microphone communications software—we connected to historical archives put online by the Davidson Library at the University of California, Santa Barbara. In the notation "Magna Carta, 1215

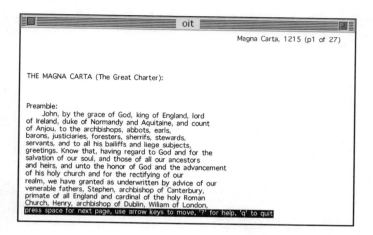

(p1 of 27)," the use of the abbreviation p, for page, is a little misleading. There is no paper, there are no pages. What the notation means is that the entire file will take up twenty-seven screens. Someone reaching the same document from a different tool, say a graphic web browser, will not see the notation.

The easiest way to cite this reference is to use the n. pag. (no pages) abbreviation in your citation. However, if you or a teacher feels it is important that you narrow down the location of a reference, the most consistent form to use is to count the paragraphs in the document. We recommend this even though you may, as in the example, have some indication that approximates pages. But recall that not everyone shares your approximation. Things can get even more complicated than just changing types of web browsers. If you access the same information by Gopher, things look different. See the example on page 158.

There, you notice the length measurement is given in percentages. You also see there are fewer lines in the window (twelve instead of thirteen). The pagination does not match even though the user accessed the Internet with the same software (Microphone on a Macintosh). Gopher and the WWW each present the same information differently. All these variables make the kind of precise citation used in print resources impossible to match. The one feature likely to be consistent for different platforms displaying the same document is the arrangement and number of paragraphs.

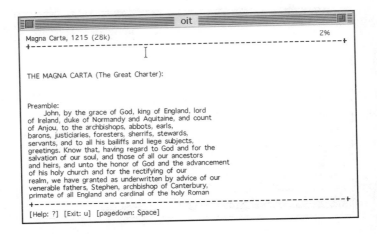

Indicate Correct Citation Particulars When Using a Downloaded File

Sometimes you must download a file and read it on your own word processor. It could be you are pressed for time, or the file might not be formatted to be read online. When you download a file, you might change how the text is laid out. Changes can be caused by such things as whether you double space, whether you reformat the text to remove paragraph returns at the end of each line, and whether you decide to print and in what font size. If you plan to make any of these changes for the purposes of ease of reading, you should do so with a copy of the file. You should then refer to the original downloaded file to indicate citation particulars. Most users who download a file will see approximately the same text layout. You can refer to the original file and find the matching portion of it simply by using the computer's ability to search for particular words and phrases.

16.3 Citation Guidelines

Most English literature and writing journals favor the Modern Language Association (MLA) in-text citation method. Some require the American Psychological Association (APA) in-text citation method. And a few will ask for papers to be done according to *The*

Chicago Manual of Style (CMS) format for the humanities—a foot-note and bibliography method. Most handbooks for writing cours-es include examples of both the MLA and APA method. Still, there are English departments, or entire schools, that require the CMS method. In this section, we will show you examples of how to cite different Internet sources using all three methods.

Our recommendations are based on what we have seen with some modifications we believe will be helpful to those who follow your citations.

16.4 Modern Language Association (MLA) Style Guidelines

The first person we know of to present a systematic use of the MLA style for citing electronic sources is Janice R. Walker, of the University of South Florida. At the Conference on College Composition and Communication held in Washington, D.C., in March 1995, the Alliance for Computers and Writing (ACW) voted to endorse Walker's "MLA-Style Citations of Electronic Sources," and built a link (http://www.cas.usf.edu/english/walk-er/mla.html) to her guide in the ACW web page. Walker's guide has guided us.

Creating a Works-Cited Entry

The principles involved in these citations are straightforward and consistent. Here's the order of elements for the works-cited entry:

1. Author's full name, last name first.
2. "Title of work" (for articles in journals, magazines, or anthologies).
3. <u>Title of work</u> (for journals, magazines, books, or antholo-gies).
4. Date source was published: number of pages or paragraphs if citing an online journal. If pages or paragraphs not used, put n. pag. for no pagination (if originally published in print; use print publication date).
5. Say it was on the Internet.
6. Internet publisher if applicable.
7. Internet protocol (MOO, Telnet, FTP).

8. Internet address.
9. Path at that address.
10. Date accessed by you.

All these elements are arranged in a format that begins by matching a standard MLA entry, then goes on to include the Internet particulars. There's a wrinkle here you should be aware of. In the few examples there are for Internet sources with MLA guidelines in 1995 English handbooks, the MLA examples have the word *Online* appear in the citation between the *Title of Work* and the Date. We do not use that here because the word *Internet* means that the work is online—but not everything that is online is on the Internet.

Last Name, First Name. "Title of Piece." Title of Work.
    Date: Possible Pagination Reference. Internet.
    [Protocol and address], [path] (date of access).

Before we go on to our examples of works-cited entries, here are a few notes about writing the in-text citation.

Working Citations into Your Text

Most of the time when you use the MLA, you will use parenthetical citations in the text of your essay to key a reader to the fact that you're referencing something. If you check an English handbook's MLA sample paper and citation examples, you'll see that the parentheses will enclose an author's last name and the page number for the reference (name #). When you are working with Internet sources that do not have page numbers, which will be many of them, substitute a paragraph number. However, make sure you indicate it is a paragraph number you are referring to. Thus instead of (name #), you would use (name paragraph #).

MLA Style for E-Mail

Personal E-Mail

Give the author's name (if known), the subject line from the posting in quotation marks, and note that it is personal mail. Unless otherwise indicated, date refers to date of the message.

Pleiske, Mary. "Teaching About AIDS."Personal e-mail
    (24 April 1994).

E-Mail from a Discussion List—Archived

For mail from an archived list, put the subject line of the message
in quotes, and underline the name of the list or archive. Think of
the relationship like this: message is to article as list name is to
name of magazine. The date after the archive name should be the
date the message was written. The date in parentheses is the date
the archive was accessed.

Wood, Wini. "Re: Alliance Gopher standards (FWD)."
    <u>Alliance for Computers and Writing List (ACW-L)</u>
    <u>Archives</u>. 17 July 1995. Internet. World Wide Web:
    http://www.ttu.edu/lists/acw-l/9407/0017.html
    (25 August 1995).

E-Mail from a Discussion List—Nonarchived

Give the name of the list, then the address used to send a message
to the list. Sometimes the list name and the name before the @
will be the same. Sometimes they will be a name and an acronym
(for example, Megabyte University and MBU-L). Sometimes, as in
the sample shown, they will be similar, but different. The date in
parentheses is the date of the message.

Earnshaw, Catherine. "Oh What Heights We'll Hit."
    Internet. Rhetnet-L, Rhetnt-l@mizzou1.missouri.edu
    (1 April 1995).

Message or File from E-Mail Program

Here the first date, March 1995, refers to the most recent update
to the guide. The second date at the end of the reference is the
date of access. Note also that both the Listserv address and message sent to the listserv software are given.

Corio, Ron, Sokolik, M., & Lee, A. "APA Style Guide"
    (ver 2.1, March 1995). Internet. E-mail:
    listserv@cmsa.berkeley.edu, message: Get TESLEJ-L
    APAGUIDE TESLEJ-L F=MAIL (18 April 1995).

E-Mail from a USENET Group

> Twain, Mark. "Re: Rumors of My Death." Internet.
> USENET: misc.writing (13 September 1995).

E-Mail Sent Inside a MOO or MUD

A participant in a MOO or MUD (see Chapter 11) is called a player. Players often take names that are short versions of their real name (like Nickc for Nick Carbone) or that are more fanciful. In MOOs and MUDs, people are known first by their player names, and second, if at all, by their real names. Sometimes a real name can be revealed by typing **@whois** or **profile** followed by the player name. Or sometimes a player will include his or her real name in a self-description. If you know or can learn the person's real name, use it in parentheses. Or you can use the person's real name (last name first, first name last), and enclose his or her player name in parentheses if the paper is more formal. Underline or italicize the name of the MOO or MUD.

Sometimes within a MOO or MUD, there are e-mail discussion groups. If a message comes from such a distribution list, include the name of the list in italics as well. The examples shown are from our imaginary MOO. MOO and MUD addresses are always given as Telnet even though users can also access them by clients. Mail sent within a MOO or MUD is often called MOO-mail or MUD-mail instead of just e-mail.

> Traveler (Jones, Tom). "No Room at the Inn." Personal e-mail in SomeMOO. Internet. Telnet:
> moo.somemoo.com 7777 (24 August 1995).

MOO or MUD E-Mail Distribution List

> Mehitabel. "When I Ruled the Nile." Governance List in SomeMOO. Internet. Telnet: moo.somemoo.com
> 7777 (14 July 1993).

MLA Style for File Transfer Protocol

You'll note in this example for Brendan Kehoe's classic *Zen and the Art of the Internet*, which we recommend, that there is a revision number. The date happens to be the date of the revision. This work is periodically updated. Note that the FTP address (ftp.internic.net) and the directory path (pub/Internet-doc/zen.txt) are separated by a comma. Commas are not part of Internet addresses. Slashes (/) and periods (.) are, so you do not want to use them to separate parts of the address and path information; it would be confusing.

> Kehoe, Brendan. "Zen and the Art of the Internet: A Beginner's Guide to the Internet," rev. 1.0. 2 February 1992. Internet. FTP: ftp.internic.net, pub/Internet-doc/zen.txt (2 February 1994).

MLA Style for Gopher

The Internet has many reference works online that have searchable databases. You should begin the citation as you would their print corollaries. In the following example, we use *The ACRONYMs Dictionary*, a work, unlike *The American Heritage Dictionary*, that is not well known. Therefore, MLA convention requires a full citation, and that is what we begin with. Had the source been more familiar, say a public domain copy of *Roget's Thesaurus*, we would begin the entry with the word we looked up and cited—no reference to the author would be needed. The date in our example comes from a file titled "About ACRONYMs Dictionary"; no publisher is associated with the dictionary. If you use a searchable database online, you will often find an "about" file for it. Read it. It will usually have important information about how to use the resource and how it came to be online. For example, in the about file for *The ACRONYMs Dictionary*, we learned it exists solely because David Sill compiled 6,000 acronyms and put them in a searchable database.

> Sill, David. "Laser." The ACRONYMs Dictionary. 15 February 1993. Internet. Gopher: info.mcc.ac.uk, port: 70, select: 1/miscellany/acronyms (3 June 1995).

You might recall from Chapter 7 that we used this example when showing you how to use Gopher's command for opening a connection to another server. Our Gopher entry differs from that used by Walker in how we present the path details. Walker recommends placing the Gopher address and path in one stream, similar to a URL entry. Her version of the address and path would be gopher: info.mcc.ac.uk/miscellany/acronyms. We recommended the change in our example for two reasons.

First, when you use the ^ command in Gopher to reveal the link information about your source, you will receive it as host, port, and path. We wanted to keep the same breakdown in the citation to make it as consistent as possible with the Gopher server software's information. This brings us to our second reason. As we noted, most of the time the port will be 70 in Gopher. However, when it is not, a user will need to know that so that he or she can erase the default and type in the correct port number. Breaking down the Gopher citation to include the port provides a way to give the correct port. The word *select* for the path corresponds to the dialog box's "selector (optional)" line.

MLA Style for the World Wide Web

Web citations will soon become very common. The technology that makes the Web possible is making it easier to do more online, drawing in more scholars and resources. In a few years, there will probably be an explosion of literary and critical journals that start web pages. Even though many people will automatically recognize that an address belongs to the Web, we still recommend that you label it as such. The Internet is still new enough that the more details you can provide your readers, the better. Further, the Web can have addresses with Gopher, FTP, and Telnet links, among others. Those links use the words *Gopher*, *FTP*, and *Telnet* in the command. Thus, for now, you should announce the protocol clearly, even when it seems obvious.

> Slade, Robert M. "Book Review: Netiquette by Virginia Shea." Computer Mediated Communication Magazine. October 1994. Internet. World Wide Web: http://sunsite.unc.edu/CMC/mag/1994/oct/netiquette.html (30 October 1994).

MLA Style for MOOs and MUDs and Other Telnet Sites

MOO or MUD Writings

This example is from our imaginary MOO. In the example, we wanted to show you how to cite a document in a MOO instead of e-mail. After the Telnet address for the MOO, you should type the room the document is in with the **@go** command before it; then give the name of the file and how to get it. In this example, Hawkins has a file visitors can read called welcome. The command to read in a MOO is **read**.

> Pirate (Hawkins, Jim). "Welcome to My Island." <u>SomeMOO.</u>
> Internet. Telnet: moo.somemoo.com 7777, @go sil-
> ver's_lair, read welcome (3 January 1993).

MOO or MUD Discussions: Planned and Unplanned

If you want to cite someone you talked to online, first make sure you have his or her permission. Quoting someone you talk to without permission is akin to secretly tape recording a conversation. It may not be illegal all the time, but it is certainly unethical. Always ask before citing a conversation in a formal paper or presentation.

With computers, it is very easy to log your online activity. You can create a log file that puts a copy of everything on your screen into a file on your computer or diskette. In these files, everything you see on-screen, including commands, error messages, intended text, and comments written by someone else in a discussion, will be saved to your log file. Many MOO, MUD, IRC clients include a log feature. You can create a file that will log that session. There are many legitimate reasons to log what you do, and you don't have to tell everyone every time you are logging. But if you do decide to quote a person (with whom you conversed), contact him or her and get permission. If it's a MOO or MUD and he or she is a regular player, MOO or MUD mail is a good way to reach the person.

Be honest about the circumstances of the discussion. If it's an interview, call it that. But if you just happened to log in and find an interesting discussion, then thank serendipity and acknowledge that in your reference. Don't inflate the conditions of the meeting to make it sound more formal for the sake of the paper. If what was said is worth having in your paper, then you should not embellish how you discovered it. Even though comments you cite may not be logged, give the directions to the room in which they occurred.

Planned Interview

> Pirate (Hawkins, Jim). "Personal Interview conducted in SomeMOO." Internet. Telnet: moo.somemoo.com 7777, @go castaway beach (4 July 1994).

Nonplanned Meeting

> Pirate (Hawkins, Jim). "Remark made in SomeMOO." Internet. Telnet: moo.somemoo.com7777, @go cas-away beach (4 July 1994).

Discussion from a Public Log

Some MOO or MUD meetings are logged, such as class meetings, planning sessions for collaborative projects, and scholarly discussions. Usually if there's a log, a title is associated with the meeting. Make sure you note that in your reference. In the following example, the title is the name of the class. Note that the directions to the log are given and not the directions to the MOO. There's a date for the archive document and a second date for when you accessed the archive.

> Pirate (Hawkins, Jim). "Remark in English 341: Sea Fictions." Class Meeting in SomeMOO: Melville Room. Internet. 9 September 1994. World Wide Web: http://www.somemoo.com/logs/english/melville/090994.txt (1 September 1995).

Telnet to an Online Database

More and more databases are coming online and are available through the Internet. Some, such as the *Oxford English Dictionary* or *InfoTrak* are licensed, and only students who attend the college or university holding the license can access them. Other databases, however, are accessible online. You'll recall from Chapter 6 that we accessed Harvard's Online Library Information Service (HOLLIS). HOLLIS allows you to search the Educational Resources Information Center (ERIC) database. If there's an essay in ERIC you want, and it comes with an ERIC Document number (ED in the following citation), you can order a copy from the nearest

ERIC repository. Or, if you attend a university or college that is an ERIC repository, you can read the microfiche.

This citation for a paper presented at an academic conference begins as if for a lecture. (Still, use the term *paper* in the citation when referring to a conference.) However, since you weren't at the lecture, you will not have the date the author spoke, or "gave her paper" as they say at academic conferences. Therefore, give the dates of the conference. After that, name the service you used (HOLLIS), how you accessed it (Internet. Telnet: 128.103.151.247 3006), the database used at the service (ERIC), and the database document details (ED number). You do not need to give your date of access. Spell out HOLLIS—it is not common enough yet to abbreviate—but you can abbreviate ERIC.

> Daisley, Margaret. "A Letter to My Mother." Paper. National Council of Teachers of English Annual Meeting. Louisville, KY, 18-23 November 1992. Harvard Online Library Information Service. Internet. Telnet: 128.103.151.247 3006, ERIC, ED 355549.

16.5 American Psychological Association (APA) Style Guidelines

The groundwork for developing our sample APA guidelines comes from Ron Corio and Maggi Sokolik, who, with help from Abraham Lee, wrote APA guidelines for the online journal *Teaching English as a Second Language—Electronic Journal*. Their guidelines can be accessed by addressing an e-mail message to listserv@cmsa.berkeley.edu, leave the subject line blank, and for a message write: get teslej-l apaguide teslej-l f=mail.

Before going into examples, we'd like to give a brief overview of the APA method. Again, for fuller details, you should check an English handbook, most of which offer thorough coverage of the APA method. APA citation elements follow this order:

1. Last name of author, followed by first initial (full first names only used if two authors in one citation have both same last name and same first initials).

2. Date, in parentheses, followed by a period.
3. Title of a work, underlined or italicized, followed by an underlined or italicized period. Only first word in title, first word of subtitles, and proper names are capitalized. (In e-mail, subject lines will be title of work; they will be underlined or italicized).
4. Titles of articles, or the equivalent of articles, within larger works are not underlined. See APA style for the World Wide Web on page 254 for example.
5. Place of publication followed by a colon, then name of publisher, period.

Here's an APA entry for a book:

Katsh, E. A. (1989). <u>The electronic media and the transformation of law.</u> New York: Oxford University Press.

Note the difference for a work in a journal or magazine. As you see, the article title will be capitalized by first letter and proper names only, the journal title will be underlined or italicized, each word capitalized.

Diegmueller, K. (1995, September). Expletives deleted. <u>Teacher Magazine,</u> 24-29.

We want to especially call your attention to the details on the dates and titles. You will need to follow the convention in your online sources. Further, the APA frowns on citing sources that others cannot access. Therefore, if you wish to use APA for unarchived e-mail or MOO meetings, you need only to mention them in text as a personal communication: "In a discussion on SomeMOO, Carrot-Top said salads give him the shivers." If you want to cite e-mail sent to you, and you think it might be important for other researchers to have, you need to get permission from the sender to save a copy and to give it to those who write you about it: you will have to note in the citation that you will make the message available. This can be cumbersome for you. If you come to such a case, the best thing is to make the message an appendix to the article. Still, let's make the unlikely our first example.

APA Style for E-Mail

You see that citing unarchived e-mail can be cumbersome. You need to not only give the name of the message as the underlined or italicized title, but you must include a bracket to explain that it was e-mail sent to you. In the TESLEJ-L APAGUIDE, Corio, Sokolik, and Lee use the term *Online* in brackets. We recommend the term *Internet*; it is more specific. The APA is still evolving their Internet guidelines; however, for other electronic sources, such as CD-ROMs, they name the medium. Naming the Internet is more consistent with this since "online" means anything done on a computer. The more specific, we believe, especially in this, the better off your readers will be.

> Brooke, D. (1995, March 15). <u>Mid-March hare: a recipe</u> [e-mail to Nick Carbone], [Internet]. Available e-mail: nickc@english.umass.edu.

Message or File from E-Mail Program

> Corio, R., Sokolik, M., & Lee, A. (1995, July). <u>APA style guide, ver. 2.2.</u> [Internet]. Available e-mail: listserv@cmsa.berkeley.edu Message: Get TESLEJ-L APAGUIDE TESLEJ-L F=MAIL.

E-Mail Message Available from an Archive

> Wood, W. (1994, July 21). <u>Re: Alliance gopher standards</u> (fwd). [Internet]. Available: Alliance for Computers and Writing List (ACW-L) Archives: World Wide Web URL: http://www.ttu.edu/lists/acw-l/9407/0017.html.

E-Mail from a USENET Group

> Twain, Mark. (1994, October 31). <u>Re. rumors of my death.</u> [Internet]. Usenet: misc.writing. Available from nick@english.umass.edu.

E-Mail from a MOO

Traveler (Jones, Tom). (1995, August 24). <u>No room at the inn.</u> [Internet]. E-mail on SomeMOO. Telnet: MOO.somemoo.com 777. Available from nick@english.umass.edu.

Papers from a MOO

Give the access date for MOO papers; they may later be moved or removed. You need to think of a MOO as an organism, one that grows and changes over time. Your date of access—the date you logged into the MOO and read the paper—alerts readers that there may be a difference between what you cite and what you find.

Pirate (Hawkins, Jim). (1993, January 3). <u>Welcome to my island.</u> Paper in SomeMOO: Silver's Lair.[Internet]. Available: Telnet MOO.somemoo.com 7777, @go silver's lair, read welcome. Accessed on January 3, 1993.

Interviews and Meetings from a MOO

In a MOO, people often use a character or player name as their online persona. You may know their real name, but if you do you can use it if it is appropriate to your paper. Or, you may use a combination of their character name and real name. It depends on the nature of the meeting. If you arrange to interview someone named Jim Hawkins in a MOO, then you would use Jim Hawkins. If you happen to run into a character named Pirate while in the MOO and he says something you want to use, then use Pirate.

If the interview is planned, you should make a log:

Pirate (Hawkins, Jim). (1993, April, 2). Interview in SomeMOO: Silver's Lair. [INTERNET]. Telnet: MOO.somemoo.com 7777, @go silver's lair. Transcript available from nick@english.umass.edu.

As you can see from the final three examples for FTP, Gopher, and the WWW, after the name of the source is given with full titles, the pattern is:

[Internet]. Available protocol: details

APA

HELPFUL HINT: You'll notice that in all the MOO examples I've indicated the transcript is available. This is because the APA frowns on citing sources with no transcripts. If you did not have a transcript, you would have to work the source into your paper without including a citation for it in the works-cited entry. You could write in your paper, "In a chance online meeting in Silver's Lair, his room on SomeMOO, Jim Hawkins, who uses the character name Pirate 'treasure maps are the key to a rollicking adventure.'"

APA Style for File Transfer Protocol

Kehoe, B.P. (1992). <u>Zen and the art of the Internet 2nd.Rev.</u> [Internet]. Available: Anonymous FTP: quake.think.com Directory: pub/etext/1992 File: Zen10.txt.

APA Style for Gopher

In the APA, the Gopher parts are named directory and filename. The TESLEJ-L APAGUIDE did not include the port. We do because every once in a while, the port will not be 70; this allows a place for those times.

Electronic Frontier Foundation (EFF). (1993). <u>Big dummy's guide to the Internet.</u> [INTERNET]. Available Gopher: vega.lib.ncsu.edu Port: 70 Directory: library/reference/guides File: Guide.txt.

APA Style for the World Wide Web

Slade, R. M. (1994, October). Review of the book <u>Netiquette Computer Mediated Communication Magazine, 2.</u> [Internet]. Available: World Wide Web, http://sunsite.unc.edu/CMC/mag/1994/oct/ netiquette.html.

16.6 *The Chicago Manual of Style* (CMS) Guidelines

Although the examples that follow are based on the most recent (fourteenth) edition of *The Chicago Manual of Style,* the editors of that volume also write that the "proliferation of documents created, stored, and disseminated on computer systems and the burgeoning requirement to cite such documents" (633) means that creating "a uniform system of citing electronic documents" (633) is still ongoing. As a practical matter, this means you will be working with sources for which the International Standards Organization (ISO—the body that guides The University of Chicago Press in these issues) has yet to devise a citation method. The examples in this section are based on our attempt to approximate *The Chicago Manual of Style* guidelines.

Most students who use the Chicago style refer to Kate L. Turabian's *A Manual for Writers of Term Papers, Theses, and Dissertations,* which is published by the University of Chicago Press. If you are required to use the Chicago style, you should refer to this book for more information, including details on the difference between the footnote and bibliography method and the in-text citation method for citing sources. In general, the in-text guidelines are used by the sciences, and the footnote and bibliography system by the humanities.

We give examples for both footnote and bibliographic entries. For in-text citation examples, we provide only the work-cited entry. In the in-text citation format, a parenthetical reference is used instead of a footnote. In the Chicago style, the parenthetical reference includes the author, the date, and the page number. Where page numbers are available, the citation will look like this (Crump and Carbone 1996, 7). In lieu of page numbers for some of your sources, you may need paragraph numbers. When you are referencing a source where paragraph numbers are used, preface the number with word *paragraph.* If you don't, your readers will assume you are referencing a page number. For example, (Slade 1994, paragraph 3) refers to Robert

Slade who in 1994 wrote a review in *Computer Mediated Communication Magazine,* an online magazine. The work-cited entry for this reference is:

Slade, Robert M. 1994. "Book Review: <u>Netiquette</u> by Virginia Shea." <u>Computer Mediated Communication Magazine,</u> October. (INTERNET). Available World Wide Web, URL: http//sunsite.unc.edu/CMC/mag/ 1994/oct/netiquette.html .

The Chicago Manual of Style recommends that titles and names of computer documents appear with the same capitalization as they do in the source document. This will mean your titles will not have the relatively uniform look they get with MLA or APA. You will also note that the in-text citation format is nearly identical to APA style in its arrangement of elements.

Computer Information Services and Databases

References to information found in online services such as ERIC (Educational Resources Information Center) or MEDLIT (Medical Literature) often consist of articles already printed in a journal or read at an academic conference. Therefore, when citing a reference you found through one of these services, first write the bibliography for it as though you had found it in the original source. Next, you append the name of the service, the name of the vendor providing the information to the service, and identify the numbers the service assigns to the article.

Note the difference between footnote and bibliography entries. Commas become periods after the author's name and the paper's title in the bibliography. The logic is to give the citation as it would appear for a paper source, then to note the service—HOLLIS, in this example—its Internet and Telnet address, and then the online database (ERIC) and database numbers—(ED#).

CMS

Footnote

1 Margaret Daisley, <u>A Letter to My Mother</u>, paper presented at the annual meeting of the National Council of Teachers of English, Louisville, KY, 18-23 November 1992. HOLLIS, (Internet), Telnet: 128.103.151.247 3006,/ERIC, ED 355549.

Bibliography

Daisley, Margaret. <u>A Letter to My Mother</u>. Paper presented at the annual meeting of the National Council of Teachers of English, Louisville, KY, 18-23 November 1992. HOLLIS, (Internet). Telnet: 128.103.151.247 3006. ERIC, ED 355549.

Work Cited

Daisley, Margaret. 1992. <u>A Letter to My Mother</u>. Paper presented at the annual meeting of the National Council of Teachers of English, Louisville, KY, 118-23 November. HOLLIS, (Internet). Telnet: 128.103.151.247 3006./ERIC, ED 355549.

CMS Style for E-Mail

Remember, some distribution lists archive their messages, but many do not; when you first join a list, read and save the welcoming files that tell you how to get off a list, how to send a message, and other details about the list. These messages will usually tell you if the list is archived. Some lists also keep a file of frequently asked questions (FAQs), which are good to review for details on list archives. Some people save copies of what they send, some do not. Depending on the significance of what you are referencing, you might do well to save a full copy of the original message as you received it, with all headers in place, on a disk, and be willing to make it available should someone request to see it.

In all e-mail examples, the last part of the reference includes the word *INTERNET*. Since there are a number of places that people use e-mail—America Online (AOL), Prodigy, and CompuServe, to name a few—it's important to know which network the mail was received on or is stored on. People on AOL, Prodigy, and CompuServe can send e-mail to the Internet, they have Internet access, but they are members of their particular online service and have access to resources nonmembers do not have. If you were to cite a source only available to a member of the service, you need to make sure you use the name of the service (COMPUSERVE, for example), instead of INTERNET. The online source appears in all capital letters. The CMS used ONLINE in their closest example to this; we recommend INTERNET for its specificity.

HELPFUL HINT: E-mail titles are determined by the subject line of the message, thus they may have varied and creative spellings and uses of capitalization. You will notice we include how often the archive is updated as well as the date the message was posted to the list. If there is an archive, reference the archive's location since that is the most reliable means for someone to find the same message.

Personal E-Mail

Footnote

1 Mary Pleiske, "Teaching About AIDS," e-mail, 24 April 1994, available from nickc@english.umass.edu; INTERNET.

Bibliography

1 Pleiske, Mary. "Teaching About AIDS." E-mail. 24 April 1994. Available from nickc@english.umass.edu; INTERNET.

Work Cited

Pleiske, Mary. 1994. Teaching About AIDS. E-mail. 24 April 1994. Available from nickc@english.umass.edu; INTERNET.

Archived E-Mail

Footnote

[1] Wini Wood, "Re: Alliance Gopher standards (FWD)," from Alliance for Computers and Writing List (ACW-L) [Listserv e-mail discussion group], ACW-L Archives, Texas Tech. University, (updated daily, posted 21 July 1994), available via World Wide Web at http://www.ttu.edu/ lists/acw-1/9407/0017.html; INTERNET.

In the preceding example, rather than have the address run on two lines, it is clearer to keep it on a single line so that there is no confusion of its elements. Some addresses will be too long. If so, never break an address before slash (/) marks, break immediately after the slash as in the example below.

Bibliography

Wood, Wini. "Re: Alliance Gopher standards (FWD)." From Alliance for Computers and Writing List (ACW-L) [Listserv e-mail discussion group]. ACW-L Archives, Texas Tech. University, (updated daily, posted 21 July 1994). Available via World Wide Web at http://www.ttu.edu/ lists/acw/9407/0017.html; INTERNET.

Work Cited

Wood, Wini. 1994. Re: Alliance Gopher standards (FWD). From Alliance for Computers and Writing List (ACW-L) [Listserv e-mail discussion group]. ACW-L Archives, Texas Tech. University, (updated daily, posted 21 July 1994). Available via World Wide Web at http://www.ttu.edu/lists/acw/9407/0017. html; INTERNET.

Message or File from E-Mail Program

Here, the first date, July 1995, refers to the date of the most recent update to the guide; the second date, at the end of the reference, is the date of access.

Footnote

¹ Ron Corio, Maggi Sokolik, & Abraham Lee, "APA STYLE
GUIDE," (ver 2.2, July 1995), (accessed on 18 April
1995), available e-mail: listserv@cmsa.berkeley.edu,
message get TESLEJ-L APAGUIDE TESLEJ-L F=MAIL;
INTERNET.

Bibliography

Corio, Ron, Sokolik, Maggi, and Lee, Abraham. "APA
STYLE GUIDE," (ver. 2.1, July 1995). [Accessed on
18 April 1995]. Available e-mail:
listserv@cmsa.berkeley.edu; Message: get TESLEJ-L
APAGUIDE TESLEJ-L F=MAIL; INTERNET.

Work Cited

Corio, Ron, Sokolik, Maggi, and Lee, Abraham. 1995.
APA STYLE GUIDE, (ver. 2.1, March 1995).
[Accessed on 18 April 1995]. Available e-mail: list-
serv@cmsa.berkeley.edu; Message: get TESLEJ-L
APAGUIDE TESLEJ-L F=MAIL; INTERNET.

E-Mail from a Discussion List—Nonarchived

Footnote

¹ Catherine Earnshaw, "Oh What Heights We'll Hit,"
Rhetnet-L, (1 April 1995), Rhetnt-l@mizzou1.mis
souri.edu; INTERNET.

Bibliography

Earnshaw, Catherine "Oh What Heights We'll Hit."
Rhetnet-L. (1 April 1995). Posted to Rhetnt-L@miz-
zou1.missouri.edu; INTERNET.

Work Cited

Earnshaw, Catherine. 1995. Oh What Heights We'll Hit.
Rhetnet-L. (1 April 1995). Posted to Rhetnt-L@miz-
zou1.missouri.edu; INTERNET.

CMS

E-Mail from a USENET Group

Footnote

> [1] Mark Twain, "Re: Rumors of My Death," USENET: misc.writing (31 October 1994). INTERNET.

Bibliography

> Twain, Mark. "Re: Rumors of My Death." USENET: misc.writing (31 October 1994). INTERNET.

Work Cited

> Twain, Mark. 31 October 1994. Re: Rumors of My Death. USENET: misc.writing. INTERNET.

E-Mail Sent Inside a MOO or MUD

A participant in a MOO or MUD is called a player. Players take names that are short versions of their real name (like Nickc for Nick Carbone) or that are more fanciful. In MOOs and MUDs, people are known first by their player names, and second, if at all, by their real names. Sometimes a real name can be revealed by typing **@whois** or **profile** followed by the player name. Or sometimes a player will include his or her real name in self-description or elsewhere. If you know the real name and get permission to use it from the player, use it in parentheses. MOOs and MUDs vary. Some people will not want their real name associated with their player name.

Footnote

> [1] Traveler (Tom Jones,), "No Room at the Inn," e-mail on SomeMOO, 24 August 1995, Telnet: MOO.somemoo.com 7777; INTERNET.

Bibliography

> Traveler (Jones, Tom). "No Room at the Inn." E-mail on SomeMOO. 24 August 1995. Telnet: MOO.somemoo.com 7777; INTERNET.

Work Cited

> Traveler (Jones, Tom). 1995. No Room at the Inn. E-mail
> on SomeMoo. Telnet: MOO.somemoo.com 7777;
> INTERNET.

MOO or MUD Discussion

MOO and MUD discussions can occur with some structure, say,
as part of an online class, a planned meeting among colleagues,
or a regular series of discussions. Discussions may or may not be
formally logged. Some logs are available only to the participants
in the discussions. Or you might make a private log of your own.
You should refer to a log only if it is publicly available.
Depending on the length of your writing or type of research, you
might include the log as an appendix, or, if you are creating a
hypertext or hypermedia presentation, you might include a link
to the log.

Footnote

> [1] Painted (Dorian Gray), online discussion, in SomeMOO:
> Artist Studio (3 May 1993), Telnet: MOO.somemoo.com
> 7777, @go Artist Studio; INTERNET.

Bibliography

> Painter (Gray, Dorian). Online discussion in SomeMOO:
> Artist Studio (3 May 1993). Telnet: MOO.somem-
> oo.com 7777. @go Artist Studio; INTERNET.

Work Cited

> Painter (Gray, Dorian). 3 May 1993. Online discussion in
> SomeMOO: Artist Studio. Telnet: MOO.someone.com
> 7777, @go Artist Studio; INTERNET.

MOO and MUD Papers, Posters, Slides, and Other Neat Stuff

MOOs and MUDs, in addition to allowing people to talk in one of
the "rooms" in their program, allow people to leave things in the

room. Objects can be created—robots that can give directions; slides (of prewritten text, such as a series of questions for discussion) that can be displayed to everyone in the room; or papers, often called posters, that can be read. To cite these things, use the following format: name of creator of object; type of object; MOO or MUD and room object is in; date accessed by you (generally, these items are not dated or given version numbers; however, if they happen to be [a MOO or MUD newspaper is a notable instance], include that as well); directions to the MOO or MUD; MOO or MUD command needed to get to the room; the command needed to read, view, activate, or use the referenced item; and the name of the network (usually this will be INTERNET) the MOO or MUD is on.

Footnote

[1] Pirate (Jim Hawkins), <u>Welcome to My Island,</u> paper in SomeMOO: Silver's Lair, (accessed on 3 January 1993), Telnet: MOO.somemoo.com 7777, @go silver's lair, read welcome; INTERNET.

Bibliography

Pirate (Hawkins, Jim). <u>Welcome to My Island.</u> Paper in SomeMOO: Silver's Lair. (accessed on 3 January 1993). Telnet: MOO.somemoo.com 7777; @go silver's lair; read welcome; INTERNET.

Work Cited

Pirate (Hawkins, Jim). 1993. <u>Welcome to My Island.</u> Paper in SomeMOO: Silver's Lair. (accessed on 3 January 1993). Telnet: MOO.somemoo.com 7777; @go silver's lair; read welcome; INTERNET.

The commands @go silver's lair and read welcome are not written in capital letters. Because they are case-sensitive commands, they should be presented in your reference in lowercase.

MOO or MUD E-Mail Distribution List

Sometimes within a MOO or MUD, there are e-mail discussion groups where members discuss issues asynchronously, that is, without all being online at the same time. If a message comes from such a distribution list, include the name of the list underlined as well.

Footnote

[1] mehitabel, "When I Ruled the Nile," e-mail from <u>Governance List</u> on SomeMOO, (posted 14 July 1993), Telnet: MOO.somemoo.com 7777; INTERNET.

Bibliography

mehitabel. "When I Ruled the Nile." E-mail from <u>Governance List</u> on SomeMOO. (posted 14 July 1993). Telnet: MOO.somemoo.com 7777; INTERNET.

Work Cited

mehitabel. 14 July 1993. When I Ruled the Nile. E-mail from <u>Governance List</u> on SomeMOO. Telnet: MOO.somemoo.com 7777; INTERNET.

CMS Style for File Transfer Protocol

FTP is a way of logging onto a remote computer, moving among its storage space, choosing a file from it, and sending the file back to your own computer. This makes citing a page or screen a bit trickier because how your computer's word processor is set to read the file may be different from someone else's. You might have a filter that automatically converts an ASCII file into your word processor's format. Another person's word processor might not convert the ASCII, but might read it as it is. These differences will cause page breaks in different places. Unless the file indicates where the page break should be, count paragraphs and use them as a guide. We mentioned this earlier in the chapter, but remind you of it here because the CMS requires you to find a way to indicate, even if it is approximate at best, where you are referencing in the document.

Footnote

[1] Brendan Kehoe, <u>Zen and the Art of the Internet: A Beginner's Guide to the Internet,</u> rev. 1.0, 1992,

(INTERNET), available FTP: FTP.internic.Net,
Directory: pub/Internet-doc, File: zen.txt, paragraph 3.

Bibliography

Kehoe, Brendan. <u>Zen and the Art of the Internet: A
Beginner's Guide to the Internet,</u> rev. 1.0. 1992.
(INTERNET). Available FTP: FTP.internic.Net,
Directory: pub/Internet-doc, File: zen.txt.

Work Cited

Kehoe, Brendan. 1992. <u>Zen and the Art of the Internet:
A Beginner's Guide to the Internet,</u> rev. 1.0.
(INTERNET). Available FTP: FTP.internic.Net,
Directory: pub/Internet-doc, File: zen.txt.

CMS Style for Gopher

Footnote

1 Electronic Frontier Foundation (EFF), "Big Dummy's
Guide to the Internet," 1993, (INTERNET), available
Gopher: vega.lib.ncsu.edu, Directory: library/ refer-
ence/guides, File: Guide.txt, paragraph 3.

Bibliography

Electronic Frontier Foundation (EFF). "Big Dummy's
Guide to the Internet," 1993. (INTERNET).
Available Gopher: vega.lib.ncsu.edu, Directory:
library/reference/guides, File: Guide.txt.

Work Cited

Electronic Frontier Foundation (EFF). 1993. Big
Dummy's Guide to the Internet, (INTERNET).
Available Gopher: vega.lib.ncsu.edu, Directory:
library/reference/guides, File: Guide.txt.

CMS Style for the World Wide Web

Footnote

[1] Arlene Rinaldi, "The Net: User Guidelines and Netiquette," 1994, (INTERNET), available World Wide Web, http://www.fau.edu/rinaldi/arlene.html, paragraph 2.

Bibliography

Rinaldi, Arlene. "The Net: User Guidelines and Netiquette." 1994. (INTERNET). Available World Wide Web, http://www.fau.edu/rinaldi/arlene.html.

Work Cited

Rinaldi, Arlene. 1994. The Net: User Guidelines and Netiquette. (INTERNET). Available World Wide Web, http://www.fau.edu/rinaldi/arlene.html.

CMS

PART

four

RESOURCES

Chapter 17. E-Mail Lists and USENET Groups:
          Sampler
Chapter 18. Learning Online: A List of
          Resources
Chapter 19. Help with the Internet

CHAPTER 17

E-Mail Lists and USENET Groups: A Sampler

CHAPTER CONTENTS

17.1 The Directories
17.2 The Lists

17.1 The Directories

The Kovacs Directory

The best place to learn about lists for discussion is from *The Directory of Scholarly Electronic Conferences*, edited by Diane Kovacs and The Directory Team. Electronic conferences include e-mail discussion lists, online journals and newsletters, USENET groups, MOOs, and other real-time conferencing programs used by scholars. To access the Kovacs Directory, you can use the following addresses:

By the World Wide Web

http://www.n2h2.com/KOVACS/

By Gopher

Host: Gopher.usask.ca, Port: 70. Select:1/computing/Internet Information/Directorial Scholarly Electronic Conferences

Other Recommended Directories

Liszt Directory of E-Mail Discussion Groups
http://www.liszt.com

Tile.Net/Listserv reference to Internet discussion groups
http://tile.net/tile/listserv/

We highlight the following lists, many of which we first learned about in *The Kovacs Directory*, because we have either been on them at one time or heard good things about them. Our sampling is by no means exhaustive; an exhaustive list would go on for pages and would eliminate the need for you to turn to Chapter 20, "Activities for Students."

17.2 The Lists

Literature

Amlit-L listserv@mizzou1.missouri.edu
American Literature discussion list; this is a great starting place for any reading, thinking, or research you're engaged in that touches on American literature. If you're taking a course on this, join as soon as possible so that you have time to learn about the list before you participate in it.

Ansax-L listserv@wvnvm.wvnet.edu
A vibrant and eclectic array of Anglo-Saxon enthusiasts make this a highly engaging list.

CHAUCER listserv@uicvm.uic.edu
We have heard good things about this list.

ENGLMU-L listserv@mizzou1.missouri.edu
This is one of the many lists maintained by Eric. It's for discussing how English literature and writing can be taught in

electronic environments. It's a good place for students to give feedback to teachers on learning online.

KIDLIT-L listserv@bingvmb.cc.binghamton.edu
Our kids read a lot, so we find ourselves increasingly interested in children's literature. The key to children's literature, you will find, is that it must meet all the requirements we associate with the word *literature*—honesty, good writing, respect for the reader, and the ability to hold the imagination.

LITERARY listserv@UCF1VM.CC.UCF.EDU
This is a good place to go for help with literary theory, critical approaches to reading, or general literary discussions.

SFLOVERS listserv@rutvm1.rutgers.edu
According to a student who loves science fiction, this is a great list. It has a wide range of topics and explores sci-fi in all its media: television, movies, books, comics, and so on.

TWAIN-L listserv@vm1.yorku.ca
This is a very good list on Mark Twain; the discussion level is serious and thoughtful.

Writing

CREWRT-L listserv@mizzou1.missouri.edu
Started by Eric Crump, this list is designed for writing teachers and writing students, and offers a place to talk about how creative writing is taught from both the teachers' and students' points of view.

EST-L listserv@asuvm.inre.asu.edu
This is a very good list for teachers who teach English for science and technology; it takes special care to consider ESL students.

EST-SL listserv@asuvm.inre.asu.edu
This is a companion list to EST-L for students to talk about their writing. What's nice is that members of EST-L lurk on this list and are able to offer assistance. If you are doing any scientific or technical writing, this is one of the best lists you can join.

Scrnwrit listserv@tamvm1.tamu.edu
Got a great idea for a movie? Think you can write a better sitcom than what you see on TV most nights? Working on dialogue for a script in your media class? Then this is the list for you. It celebrates screenwriting and offers a great place to find kindred souls.

USENET Groups for Writing and Literature

These discussion groups about writing, words, teaching writing, and literature do not represent an exhaustive list, but they are a good place to start. If your school does not access one of these lists, contact your system administrator and ask him or her to include it in the USENET listings for the campus.

Writing Instruction

bit.listserv.mbu-l
This is Megabyte University, a discussion list for teaching writing and writing on computers.

bit.listserv.wac-l
This is Writing Across the Curriculum, a list for issues in writing for courses other than English and Composition 101.

comp.edu.composition
The Computers and Composition Digest, a service that gathers messages from different lists concerned with computers and writing.

General Writing

misc.writing
Miscellaneous writing is a deceiving name. We tend to think of "miscellaneous", as we do "etcetera" and "whatever," as an afterthought. Think of this group as a miscellany, a compendium of topics, insights, and contentions about writing from a variety of writers.

Specialized Writing

misc.writing.screenplays
Discusses both the writing and selling of screenplays.

alt.stagecraft
This group discusses technical aspects of theater production. If you're writing plays, this will be a useful resource for insight into how your work might be produced.

bit.listserv.techwr-l
Technical writing discussion list. This group has technical writers and technical writing instructors and students on it. It's a good mix of people from the professions and the schools.

alt.graffiti
Yes, a discussion of graffiti. To what extent are some pages on the WWW a kind of virtual graffiti?

The English Language

alt.usage.english
This group covers all kinds of peculiarities in English. It's entertaining because the issues almost always include some difference in interpretation of rules of usage, a sign of the vitality of the English language.

bit.listserv.words-l
A discussion of word histories, origins, and uses in English, both spoken and written.

alt.humor.puns
You might roll your eyes and wince while downloading some of these gems, but if you like wordplay, you'll want to visit this newsgroup.

Literature and Authors

bit.listserv.literary
Literary covers a wide range of topics having to do with the interpretation and enjoyment of literature. If you think of interpretation and enjoyment as separate, this list shows they are not.

Writing in Computer-Dependent Forums

comp.infosystems.www.authoring.html
Writing HTML for the World Wide Web. The questions and advice range from novice to expert. This is a good place to start learning about HTML.

alt.hypertext
For discussing issues in hypertext writing; conversation covers practice and theory.

A List for Getting Help

newbienewz

This list runs on Majordomo software. It is designed for people who are new to the Internet. You can ask any question about the Internet, including how to get connected to it, and no one will fire off an impatient RTFM flame. To subscribe, send an e-mail to NewbieNewz-request@io.com with the message **subscribe newbienewz**.

Learning Online: A List of Resources

CHAPTER CONTENTS
18.1   Searches
18.2   English Departments and Courses
18.3   Scholarly Societies
18.4   Literature and the Humanities
18.5   Writing
18.6   A Sampling of Online Writing Labs
18.7   General Education Resources
18.8   MOO and MUD Resources
18.9   Publications
18.10 Project Gutenberg
18.11 Government Resources

The Internet sites listed in this section represent only a sampling of the resources available for English majors to use. Since the study of English literature and writing can take you to a variety of subjects, this list of resources will do the same. We begin with resources for conducting searches, then move to subject-categorized databases, and from there into particular areas relevant to English majors. For Gopher-based resources, we provide the Gopher information as well as its World Wide Web URL. In Chapter 19 we list resources for learning more about the Internet, the World Wide Web, and for getting Internet tools.

18.1 Searches

Direct (or Keyword) Searches

FTP Gateways and Archie Searches
Gopher:
Host: gopher.tc.umn.edu, Port: 70, Select: 1/FTP Searches
WWW:
gopher://gopher.tc.umn.edu:70/11/FTP%20Searches

Veronica Search
This search helps you find Gopher directory titles. Useful search words might include "Shakespeare," "Literature," or "Computers and Writing."
Gopher:
Host: gopher.tc.umn.edu, Port: 70, Select: 1/Other Gopher and Information Servers/Veronica
WWW:
gopher://gopher.tc.umn.edu:70/11/
Other%20Gopher%20and%20Information%20Servers/

WAIS-Based Information
Gopher:
Host: gopher-gw.micro.umn.edu, Port: 70, Select: 1/WAISes
WWW:
gopher://gopher-gw.micro.umn.edu:70/11/WAISes

All In One Search http://www.albany.net/~wcross/all1srch.html
Allows you to search many sites—WWW, FTP servers, Gopher—by subject.

Digital's Search Program http://www.altavista.digital.com/

Lycos Search http://www.lycos.com

Metacrawler Search
http://metacrawler.cs.washington.edu:8080/index.html

WebCrawler Search http://webcrawler.com/

WWW Worm Search
http://www.cs.colorado.edu/home/mcbryan/WWWW.html

Undirected Searches
URouLette http://www.uroulette.com:8000/
Spin the wheel and go to random Web sites.

Subject-Categorized Search Resources
Subject-categorized searches take you to sites with topic or subject headings. Many of these work on a tree-branch model, starting with broad categories or topics and then narrowing the categories down in more detailed links or subdirectories. These areas are fun to browse. Remember to use your bookmarking feature if you find something you like and plan to return to.

Gopher Jewels
Gopher:
Host: cwis.usc.edu, Port: 70, Select:
1/Other_Gophers_and_Information_Resources/
Gophers_by_Subject/Gopher_Jewels
WWW:
gopher://cwis.usc.edu:70/11/
Other_Gophers_and_Information_Resources/
Gophers_by_Subject/Gopher_Jewels

PEG, a Peripatetic, Eclectic GOPHER
This is a neat place to browse; it is maintained by Calvin Boyer of the University of California-Irvine Office of Academic Computing.

Gopher:
Host: peg.cwis.uci.edu, Port: 7000, Select: 1/
gopher.welcome/peg/
WWW:
gopher://peg.cwis.uci.edu:7000/11/gopher.welcome/peg/
Notice the port is not the usual 70. Here's a list of links currently at PEG:

1. About PEG, a Peripatetic, Eclectic GOPHER
2. Biology/
3. Electronic Journals/
4. Favorite Bookmarks/

5. GOPHERS/
6. Humanities
7. INTERNET ASSISTANCE/
8. Irvine Weather and world events/
9. LIBRARIES/
10. MATHEMATICS/
11. MEDICINE/
12. PHILOSOPHY/
13. POLITICS and GOVERNMENT/
14. Physics/
15. VIRTUAL REFERENCE DESK/
16. VIRTUAL REFERENCE DESK UCI SPECIFIC/
17. WOMEN'S STUDIES and RESOURCES/

Awesome Lists http://www.clark.net/pub/journalism/
awesome.html
These are lists John Makulovich developed for journalists and
for training people on how to use the Internet. These are useful for English majors because many journalism courses fall
under English departments, and journalism, like English literature, and writing, covers many fields.

**The University of Michigan's Subject-Categorized Internet
Resources** http://www.lib.umich.edu/chhome.html

The World Wide Web Virtual Library
http://www.w3.org/hypertext/DataSources/bySubject/
Overview.html

The Yahoo Directory http://www.yahoo.com/

Webliography http://www.lib.lsu.edu/weblio.html
Steven R. Harris is a librarian at Louisiana State University. His
collection of resources is intended to be of aid to academic
searching.

Phone and E-Mail Address Books
These are especially good for finding e-mail addresses.
Gopher:
Host: gopher.tc.umn.edu, Port: 70, Select: 1/Phone Book
WWW:
gopher://gopher.tc.umn.edu:70/11/Phone%20Books

18.2 English Departments and Courses

This category of resources includes information on other online
English departments. You can do anything from investigating

graduate school programs to seeing what other students are doing on the Internet with classwork.

English and Humanities Departments On-Line
http://www.academic.marist.edu/otherdep.htm
There are a lot of collections online of English Departments and their resources and programs, but the best one we have found so far is maintained by Tom Goldpaugh, an Assistant Professor of English at Marist College.

English Departments World Wide
Gopher:
Host: gopher-server.cwis.uci.edu, Port: 7038, Select: 1/worldeng/othenggop

The Literary Research Guide's List of Online Courses
http://www.english.upenn.edu/~jlynch/syllabi.html
Syllabi for literature courses using the Internet.

Writing for the World
http://icarus.uic.edu/~kdorwick/world.html

Writing Classes on the Web
http://ernie.bgsu.edu/~skrause/WWW_Classes/

World Lecture Hall
http://www.utexas.edu/world/lecture/

Voice of the Shuttle
http://humanitas.ucsb.edu/shuttle/eng-c.html
Syllabi and teaching resources for English literature and writing courses.

18.3 Scholarly Societies

The Alliance for Computer and Writing (ACW) Home Page
http://english.ttu.edu/acw/
An excellent source for seeing what writing teachers and students are doing on the Internet; includes helpful links for beginners. As a professional organization, it also offers support to teachers, including advice, sample syllabi, software reviews, bibliographies, and conference information.

Association of Teachers of Technical Writing
http://english.ttu.edu/ATTW/

List of Home Pages of Scholarly Societies and Associations
http://www.lib.uwaterloo.ca/society/overview.html

Modern Humanities Research Association (MHRA)
http://www.hull.ac.uk/Hull/FR_Web/mhra.html
Of special use is the MHRA's ABELL: The Annual Bibliography of English Language and Literature (http://www.hull.ac.uk/Hull/FR_Web/abell.html).

Modern Language Association Graduate Student Caucus Home Page
http://www.reg.uci.edu/UCI/HUMANITIES/ENGLISH

The National Association of Graduate and Professional Students
http://www.access.digex.net/~rosati/nagps-hp.html

National Council of Teachers of English (NCTE)
http://www.note.org/

The NCTE Gopher
Host: marvin.clemson.edu, Port: 70, Select D-2:726:NCTE Gopher Server

Scholarly Information Resources
http://www.lib.lsu.edu/general/scholar.html

Writing Across the Curriculum (WAC) Home Page
http://ewu66649.ewu.edu/WAC.html

18.4 Literature and the Humanities

The American Studies Web
http://www.cis.yale.edu/~davidp/amstud.html
This is the best place to start if you're looking for Internet sources on American studies, including literature, history, culture, and politics.

A Directory of Medieval Studies Resources
http://www.georgetown.edu/labyrinth/Virtual_Library/Medieval_Studies.html
This links to archives of manuscripts, discussion lists, and articles on Medieval literature and history.

A Directory of Humanities Resources on the Internet
http://www.lib.lsu.edu/weblio.html#Humanities
This is one of the subcategories in Stephen Harris's Webliography.

The Carnegie Mellon English Server
http://english-server.hss.cmu.edu/
This resource is excellent and extensive.

A Guide to Literature on the Internet
http://www.cis.ohio-state.edu/text/faq/usenet/internet/
literary-resources/faq.html
This is a Frequently Asked Questions file about literary resources. This is a good item to scan for further ideas for searches and lists of literature FAQs for USENET groups.

Literary Research Tools on the Net
http://www.english.upenn.edu/~jlynch/lit
This is one of the most thorough and useful resources on the Internet.

18.5 Writing

Internet Writers Resource Guide from Bricolage
http://bel.avonibp.co.uk/bricolage/resources/lounge/IWRG/
index.html
An extensive guide with links to professional writer's groups, information on contracts and copyright, and genre-specific advice (children's fiction, science fiction, short story).

Writer's Resources on the Web
http://www.interlog.com/~ohi/www/writesource.html
Part of the World Wide Web Virtual Library, this page categorizes information for writers and on writing by subject. A very thorough resource.

The Word
http://www.speakeasy.org/~dbrick/Hot/word.html
An eclectic collection of links that cover writing resources, magazines, journals, and reference works.

18.6 A Sampling of Online Writing Labs

The National Writing Centers Association (NWCA)
http://www2.colgate.edu/diw/NWCA.html

The NWCA's List of Online Writing Labs and Centers
http://www2.colgate.edu/diw/NWCAOWLS.html

The CyberspaceWriting Center Consultation Project (WritingWorks)
http://fur.rscc.cc.tn.us/cyberproject

Roane State Community College
http://fur.rscc.cc.tn.us/OWL/OWL.html

Dakota State University
http://www.dsu.edu/departments/liberal/cola/OWL/

Purdue University
http://owl.trc.purdue.edu/

Texas Tech. University Writing Center
http://english.ttu.edu/UWC/UWC.html

The University of Michigan-Ann Arbor
http://www.umich.edu/~nesta/OWL/owl.html

The University of Missouri-Columbia
http://www.missouri.edu/~wleric/writery.html

The University of Oregon
http://darkwing.uoregon.edu/~jcross/word.html

The University of Texas-Austin
http://www.utexas.edu/depts/uwc/.html/main.html

18.7 General Education Resources

Educational Resources Information Center (ERIC)
ERIC is one of the leading databases and resources for education and education related articles.
Gopher:
Host: ericir.syr.edu, Port: 70, Select: 1/Clearinghouses/
16houses/CLL

WWW:
http://www.aspensys.com/eric/index.html
gopher://ericir.syr.edu:70/11/Clearinghouses/16houses/CLL

The Global Network Navigator's (GNN) Education Resources
http://gnn.com/edu/
GNN is a leader in Internet exploration and documentation.
GNN is also a service provider. Their links are among the most up to date and reliable.

18.8 MOO and MUD Resources

Diversity University MOO telnet moo.du.org 8888
Teachers can bring classes here.

CollegeTown MOO telnet patty.bvu.edu 7777
An online, college model MOO.

Connections MOO telnet oz.net 3333
A MOO for teachers and students to come as a class or on their own; friendly, supportive, and fun.

Virtual Online University telnet brazos.iac.net 8888
A liberal arts university offering courses for credit; it is a model for distance education.

VOUMOO Web Page http://www.athena.edu/index.html

University of Missouri's ZooMOO
telnet showme.missouri.edu 8888
Lots of projects by English classes.

ZooMOO Web Page http://www.missouri.edu:80/~moo/

Help for MOOs and MUDs

CMC Forums by John December
http://www.rpi.edu/Internet/Guides/decemj/itools/cmc.html
Covers MOOs, MUDs, and a whole lot more.

The MOO Central Help Page by Jeffrey R. Galin
http://www.pitt.edu/~jrgst7/MOOcentral.html
Excellent source for educational uses of MOOs, with Telnet links to a wide variety of MOOs.

Lydia Leong's Information on MUDs/MOOs/MUSHes
http://www.cis.upenn.edu/~lwl/mudinfo.html
One of the most authoritative sites; good links to research on MUDs, MOOs, and MUSHes.

18.9 Publications

Publication Directories

A Directory of Scholarly Publications
http://www.georgetown.edu/labyrinth/professional/pubs/
scholarly_pubs.html

The following links are from Carnegie Mellon's English Server:

A Directory of Online Journals and Periodicals
http://english.hss.cmu.edu/Journals.html

A Directory of Online Books by Author
http://www.cs.cmu.edu:8001/Web/bookauthors.html

A Directory of Online Books
http://www.cs.cmu.edu/Web/books.htm

Banned Books Online
http://www.cs.cmu.edu/Web/People/spok/banned-books.html
A great (and sobering) resource on censorship.

Online Reference Works
http://www.cs.cmu.edu:8001/Web/references.html

Online Journals

Kairos: A Journal for Teachers of Writing in Webbed Environments
http://english.ttu.edu/kairos/
A new online journal for teachers and students who are using the World Wide Web in writing classes.

RhetNet, a Cyberjournal for Rhetoric and Writing
http://www.missouri.edu/~rhetnet
An exploratory publication that intentionally takes the shape of the Net rather than replicating print conventions of form and content. Its contents include threads of conversation culled from mailing list discussions.

Computers and Composition, an International Journal for Teachers of Writing
http://human.www.sunet.se/cc/
The primary print journal for the computers and writing community since the mid-1980s. Back issues are being added to this web site, as well as featured articles in recent issues.

Research & Reflection: A Journal of Educational Praxis
http://www.rosauer.gonzaga.edu/~rr/rr.html

Journal of Advanced Composition
http://nosferatu.cas.usf.edu/JAC/index.html

Computer-Mediated Communication Magazine
http://www.december.com/cmc/mag/current/toc.html

Post-Modern Culture, An Electronic Journal of Interdisciplinary Criticism
http://jefferson.village.virginia.edu/pmc/contents.all.html

The Missouri Review
http://www.missouri.edu/~moreview/

The Milton Quarterly
http://voyager.cns.ohiou.edu/~somalley/milton.html

Modern Fiction Studies
http://www.sla.purdue.edu/academic/engl/mfs/

Romanticism on the Net
http://info.ox.ac.uk:80/~scat0385/

Asian Pacific Exchange Journal
gopher://naio.kcc.hawaii.edu/1D-1%3A1010%3AAPEX-J

The Bryn Mawr Classical Review
gopher://gopher.lib.Virginia.EDU/11/alpha/bmcr

The Bryn Mawr Medieval Review
gopher://gopher.lib.Virginia.EDU/11/alpha/bmmr

Seulemonde: A Journal of Culture Studies
http://nosferatu.cas.usf.edu/journal/index.html

*Teaching English as a Second Language Electronic Journal
(TESL-EJ)*
http://www.well.com/www/sokolik/index.html

The Trincoll Journal
http://www.trincoll.edu/tj/trincolljournal.html
This is written and produced by students at Trinity College in
Hartford, Connecticut.

Online Magazines

Periodicals, Magazines, and Journals
This will link you to many online journals and magazines.
Gopher:
Host: ftp.std.com, Port: 70, Select: 1/periodicals
WWW:
gopher://ftp.std.com:70/11/periodicals

The Electronic Newstand
An outlet for print journals and magazines, it offers excerpts
and sample articles. A good place to try out a journal or maga-
zine before buying a subscription.
Gopher:
Host: gopher.internet.com, Port: 70
WWW:
gopher://gopher.internet.com:70/11/

The Atlantic Monthly
http://www2.theatlantic.com/Atlantic/

Congressional Quarterly's American Voter
http://voter96.cqalert.com/

HotWired
http://www.hotwired.com/
The online companion to *Wired*, a magazine that focuses on technology and culture.

Internet World
http://pubs.iworld.com/iw-online/index.html

Mother Jones
http://www.mojones.com/
A progressive, investigative journal.

Nando.Net, a News Service from McClatchy New Media
http://www2.nando.net/

The National Review
http://pathfinder.com/@@qPIp8*I2WQIAQJCn/NR/
A conservative journal. As you can see from the URL, it is part of Time Warner's Pathfinder collection of links. It will most likely be easier to open a connection to http://pathfinder.com/ and from there click the National Review link.

The New York Times
http://www.nytimes.com/

Time Warner's Pathfinder Web News Service
http://pathfinder.com/
Links to *Time*, *Entertainment Weekly*, *People* and other magazines.

The Utne Lens
http://www.utne.com/

Who Cares Magazine
http://www.whocares.org/themag.html
An online journal of community service ideas and issues.

18.10 Project Gutenberg

The Gutenberg E-Text Home Page
http://jg.cso.uiuc.edu/PG/Welcome.html

Gutenberg Project Gopher
Gopher:

Host: spinaltap.micro.umn.edu, Port: 70, Select: 1/Gutenberg
WWW:
gopher://spinaltap.micro.umn.edu:70/11/Gutenberg

18.11 Government Resources

The Library of Congress
http://lcweb.loc.gov/
The library is in the process of digitizing some of its best collections. For example, you can access the Federal Writer's
Folklore Project interviews conducted from 1936 to 1940.

Thomas: Legislative Information
http://thomas.loc.gov/
Includes information on pending bills, committee assignments,
and homepages of representatives.

The U.S. Department of Education
http://www.ed.gov/
Great resources for learning about grants, Goals 2000, innova-
tive educational practices, and links to other education
resources.

TheVice-President's Electronic Open Meeting
http://www.npr.gov/OpenMeet/openmeet.html
An experiment in interactive government.

The White House
http://www.whitehouse.gov/
Connect to the White House and find position statements and
press releases among the information.

CHAPTER

Help with the Internet

CHAPTER CONTENTS
19.1 Online Books About the Internet
19.2 Printed Books About the Internet
19.3 Other Online Internet Guides
19.4 Help with the World Wide Web
19.5 Netiquette and E-Mail Guides
19.6 Sites for Internet Tools

This list contains resources for learning more about the Internet and the World Wide Web.

19.1 Online Books About the Internet

Daniel J. Barrett. *Bandits on the Information Superhighway.*
O'Reilly and Associates.
http://www.ora.com/gnn/bus/ora/item/bandits.html

John December. *Internet Web Text—A Guide to the Internet.*
http://www.rpi.edu/Internet/Guides/decemj/text.html

Mark Harrison. *The USENET Handbook*. O'Reilly and Associates.
http://www.ora.com/gnn/bus/ora/item/useneth.html

Tanya Herlick and Michael Bauer. *Internet Basics*.
http://www.sen.ca.gov/www/leginfo/docs/orient/
help1_intro.html

Ed Krol, adapted by Bruce Klopfenstein. *The Whole Internet
User's Guide & Catalog, Academic Edition*.
http://www.ora.com/gnn/bus/ora/item/twi2aca.html

Linda Lamb and Jerry Peek. *Using E-mail Effectively*. O'Reilly
and Associates. http://www.ora.com/gnn/bus/ora/item/use-
mail.html

David W. Sanderson. *Smileys*. O'Reilly and Associates.
http://www.ora.com/gnn/bus/ora/item/smileys.html

Victor Vitanza. *CyberReader*. Allyn and Bacon, 1996.
http://www.abacon.com/cyber/public_html/cyber.html

19.2 Printed Books About the Internet

Bill Junor and Chris DeMontravel. *Internet: The User's Guide for
Everyone*. Branden Books, 1995.

Dave Taylor. *Creating Cool Web Pages with HTML*. IDG Books,
1995.

Victor Vitanza. *CyberReader*. Allyn and Bacon, 1996.

19.3 Other Online Internet Guides

Newbie Net Internation Home Page
http://www.Newbie.NET/
"Helping anybody learn the basic skills needed to tap into the
tremendous wealth of information residing in that big virtual
thingie called the Internet is the core of our mission." The site
features a cybercourse as well as directions on how to join an
e-mail list where you can ask any, and they do mean *any*, question about using the Internet.

Computers: Internet Beginner's Guides
http://www.yahoo.com/Computers/Internet/Beginner_s_Guide/
From the Yahoo directory.

19.4 Help with the World Wide Web

HTML Tutorial—Overview
http://www-pcd.stanford.edu/mogens/intro/tutorial.html
We recommend starting here for step-by-step directions. This
resource is maintained by Christian Mogensen of Stanford
University.

WWW for Newbies
http://www.pitt.edu/~jrgst7/newbie.html
By Jeffrey R. Galin, whose pages are among the most user
friendly.

Resources for Learning About SGML & HTML
http://www.lib.lsu.edu/hum/sgml.html
Compiled by Steven R. Harris.

Maricopa Center for Learning and Instruction
http://www.mcli.dist.maricopa.edu/
A site with instructional material for those who are relatively
new to the Internet, including how-to files on creating web
documents. One of the best resources for teachers and students
on the World Wide Web.

Computers: World Wide Web Beginner's Guide
http://www.yahoo.com/Computers/World_Wide_Web/
Beginner_s_Guides/
From the Yahoo directory.

World Wide Web Consortium Homepage
http://WWW.w3.org/
Sources about writing and working in the WWW, as well as
links to useful sites.

A Timeline Tracing the Development of the Web
http://WWW.w3.org/hypertext/WWW/History.html
You'll be amazed at how far and how quickly the WWW has
developed.

**Computers and Writing Research at Lab—The University of
Texas**
http://www.en.utexas.edu/
This is an eclectic array of resources, including tutorials and
helps sheets, links to scholarly articles about teaching in computer environments, and links to student web pages. A good
place to go to see what other students are doing.

Web Style Manual from Yale University's Center for Advanced Instructional Media
http://info.med.yale.edu/caim/StyleManual_Top.HTML
This is one of the most highly recommended sources on the Internet for learning how to create and design web pages.

The World Wide Web Unleashed
http://www.rpi.edu/~decemj/works/wwwu.html
An online hypertext book by John December and Neil Randall. One of the most thorough WWW resources you'll ever find. Check out the Index when you get there.

19.5 Netiquette and E-Mail Guides

Arlene Rinaldi's Netiquette Homepage
http://www.fau.edu/rinaldi/netiquette.html
This is one of the better online netiquette guides and is frequently cited by other writers concerned with Internet citizenship.

The Unofficial Smilie Dictionary Smilies
gopher://vega.lib.ncsu.edu/00/library/reference/dictionaries/smilies
For all of your e-mail needs and emotions, sometimes referred to as emoticons.

A Beginner's Guide to Effective E-Mail
http://www.webfoot.com/advice/estyle.html
With links to other guides, gracefully written by Kaitlin Duck Sherwood.

19.6 Sites for Internet Tools

Web Browsers

Netscape Communications' Homepage
http://home.Netscape.com/

NCSA Mosaic's Homepage
http://www.ncsa.uiuc.edu/SDG/Software/Mosaic/
NCSAMosaicHome.html

TradeWave's Homepage
http://galaxy.einet.Net/EINet/EINet.html

Other Internet Tools

GIFConverter Site
http://www.kamit.com/gifconverter.html
A software tool for viewing and converting graphics. Useful for web designing or for those with nongraphic browsers who choose to download images to their own computer.

Java Site
http://www.javasoft.com/index.html
Java is a new programming language; this is for advanced users. It's in this introductory guide because if you're truly interested in learning more about the Internet for your own personal or academic use, you'll want to know about Java.

Merit Software Archives
Here you will find software for both Macintosh and PC formats.
Gopher:
Host: gopher.archive.merit.edu, Port: 70, Select: 1/
.software-archives
WWW:
gopher://gopher.archive.merit.edu:70/11/.software-archives

Washington University Archives
http://wuarchive.wustl.edu/
A huge collection of documents and software.

PART
five

ACTIVITIES

Chapter 20.   Activities for Students

CHAPTER 20

Activities for Students

CHAPTER CONTENTS
20.1 USENET for Yourself
20.2 USENET for English Classes
20.3 E-Mail Address Searches
20.4 Gopher Searching
20.5 Veronica and WAIS
20.6 Searching the Web

20.1 USENET for Yourself

We start with USENET because it offers a great way to begin using e-mail even if you do not yet have a class, a teacher, or friends using e-mail. USENET is a worldwide discussion network. Particular discussions—and there are thousands of them—form in areas called newsgroups. When you join, or subscribe, to a USENET newsgroup, you choose to have messages from that group sent to your USENET reader, a program that accesses the USENET newsgroups your provider chooses to make available. The best way to learn more about USENET is by accessing it and checking out the following newsgroups. This is your first activity.

213

1. Learn from your provider how you access USENET at your school. Make sure you learn, or get help sheets, on:
   a. How to access the newsreader.
   b. How to list all USENET groups your site allows.
   c. How to subscribe to newsgroups you want to read.
   d. How to post a message to a newsgroup as:
      1. A new message.
      2. A follow-up to a message you saw on the group.
      3. A follow-up where you can control how much of the original message is included in your follow-up.
   e. How to save messages of interest.

2. Use the command to list all the groups, and search until you find the following:

   news.announce.newusers—a newsgroup with important articles about USENET, USENET etiquette, and FAQs about using USENET.

   news.newusers.questions—a newsgroup where you can ask questions about USENET.

   news.answers—a newsgroup that lists the FAQ files for many (not all) of the newsgroups that maintain FAQs. You will want to peruse here after you have discovered a newsgroup you want to join.

   alt.Internet.services—a newsgroup where you can ask questions about using the Internet.

3. From the group news.announce.newusers, find the USENET FAQ, save it to a file on your account, and then download it to your own computer.

4. After you become familiar with the content of these newsgroups, choose one or two that discuss topics you enjoy, then join in the discussion.

20.2 USENET for English Classes

Joining a group as participant is fairly simple. Using USENET newsgroups as a basis for courses is more difficult. The information on USENET varies in quality and reliability. You can use virtually any information you come across depending, of course, on how you frame it. If you are in a writing course and are studying political rhetoric, you might choose to read alt.politics.clinton.

The messages will be contentious, even nasty, and will offer some interesting insights into how people frame an argument. The list will provide a good source of study. However, you would not want to use the same list as a source of authority on a political position. You would not want to quote someone's opinion as proof of the validity of an argument.

On the other hand, you will find USENET groups that do have experts. For an unusual example, on the newsgroup alt.books.tom-clancy, Tom Clancy frequently contributes messages. If he answers a question you have about some point in one of his books, that is a good appeal to authority to have in a paper. Not many English courses will involve reading Tom Clancy books, however. The trick in using USENET for course work is in judging the quality and worth of any particular message. Here are some useful ways to use USENET:

1. Start a conversation about what you are writing about in a paper. You may or may not want to announce you are writing about the topic; the idea here is that by discussing the ideas you have for the paper with a more diverse audience than you are likely to find in your classroom, you will get a wider range of views. This allows you to try out ideas ahead of time and to see whether you are expressing them as clearly as they need to be expressed to be understood.

2. Use groups as a way to find out what other people have read or think about the topic. If you join humanities.lit.authors.shakespeare and are writing about Hamlet, you might describe what you are trying to discern—say, how Hamlet ultimately decides the question, "To be or not to be." You might request any essays or books on Shakespeare that newsgroup members know of that might help. Here's how your request might be worded:

I'm working on an essay that tries to explain what Hamlet's answer is to the question, "To be or not to be." My argument will be that he chooses to simply, "let be." That is, he finally accepts what's before him and acts. Have any of you thought about this, and does the argument seem plausible? Also I'm interested in articles or books related to this soliloquy—I know there are going to be hundreds. Do you have any favorites that you would especially recommend?

3. Don't post a lame question like this one to humanities. lit.authors.shakespeare:

When Hamlet says "To be or not to be," what does he finally decide? I have to write an essay on "Hamlet's answer to his soliloquy." I am totally lost. Does anyone have any ideas?

4. Keep in mind that newsgroup members, though they might include teachers, are not online to teach. They join a group because they are interested in the topic. The question as posed in step 3 is framed the way you might ask a teacher during his or her office hours. It pleads and begs for help. Teachers should, and most will, hear that plea and offer more guidance, perhaps by rephrasing the assignment, or pointing the student to an essay, or suggesting some possible answers for the student to consider. Newsgroup members, however, might see the question as a nuisance, and the questioner as someone who is too lazy to try to come up with an essay on his or her own. In step 2, the same question is asked, but more specifically, without saying that it is a school assignment; further it offers readers an intimation of what the writer thinks. It's an engaged question, not a whine.

HELPFUL HINT: As a rule, never say, in a newsgroup or mailing list, that you are asking a question because you need to do so for homework or as part of a class assignment. The impression given then is that the only reason you are on the group or list is that a teacher told you to be there. All list members will remember a time when they had to do something they didn't want to do; they will assume you dislike being among them, and that you are using the members of that community only to fulfill an assignment. If you join a community, join it as a full member. Bring to it your own ideas and interest, participate, and use what information and ideas you get, making sure to carefully cite your sources.

20.3 E-Mail Address Searches

As you know by now, USENET uses e-mail. For many of you, your news reader program will include the same kind of text editor as your e-mail program. Although there is a lot of overlap in how USENET and e-mail function, it helps to think of them as separate. USENET is a particular way to use e-mail, but e-mail can be used beyond USENET.

These next few activities are ways to help you use e-mail.

1. Find out if anyone you know—family, friends, faculty—have access to and use e-mail; if they do, ask them for their e-mail address. Then send them e-mail. But before you do, learn how to create an address or alias list in your e-mail program so that you have a record of the address and aren't forever consigned to finding that scrap of paper you wrote it on. And remember, aliases make it easier to address a message.

Helpful Hint: An alias reduces the margin of error, assuming it's written correctly, because it frees you from having to type a full address. E-mail addresses are like phone numbers—one digit or character off, and you make the wrong connection or no connection.

2. If you want to surprise someone with e-mail, you can try to see if he or she has an address by asking someone else who knows the person. Or try a campus phone book. Most campus information servers will provide some means for looking up e-mail addresses of people on that campus. The easiest way to use this type of phone book is to use the WWW or Gopher to access the campus.

In the WWW, you can use a search engine such as Webcrawler or Lycos; in Gopher, you could use Veronica to search gopher-space directories. For a search word, type in the name of your friend's school. If the school has a web page or Gopher server, you'll be given a link to it; actually, you'll be given a list of links that use the words in your search. Thus if you search for Trinity

College, you'll get all sites that mention Trinity or College as separate words. You can choose search options very easily and narrow your search by clicking the All option in Webcrawler or the AND option in Lycos; in Gopher, if you are using a modem to reach your campus server, you must use BOOLean search patterns. So in Gopher searches, on your input line, you would type **Trinity AND College**. (It is important that you type AND in all capital letters.)

Once you reach the school server for your friend's college or university, browse the directories to see if there is an online phone book.

3. If you can't access the particular campus where your friend goes, or, if in doing so, you can't find his or her name and address in the campus phone books, you can attempt a Netfind search. In Gopher, use the address Gopher.tc.umn.edu. Once there, choose the Phone books menu and then choose the Other menu. If you want to access this via the WWW, you can use URL Gopher://Gopher.tc.umn.edu/11/Phone%20Books. In either case, here's what you'll find:

INTERNET-WIDE E-MAIL ADDRESS SEARCHES

(DIR) Gopher to Netfind Gateway
(FILE) Netfind search for Internet e-mail addresses overview
(TEL) Netfind server at AARNet (Melbourne, Australia)
(TEL) Netfind server at Catholic University, Santiago, Chile
(TEL) Netfind server at OpenConnect Systems, Dallas, Texas
(TEL) Netfind server at Slovak Academy of Sciences, Slovakia
(TEL) Netfind server at University of Alabama, Birmingham
(TEL) Netfind server at the University of Colorado, Boulder
(?) USENET contributor e-mail addresses
(FILE) USENET contributor e-mail addresses overview
(TEL) X.500 directory
(FILE) X.500 directory overview

The (TEL) designations let you know that if you choose the option in which they appear, you will activate a Telnet command that will take you to a remote computer where the Netfind program is stored. Remember, when you Telnet, you are asked for a login name. To use Netfind the login name is netfind.

Once in, follow the directions. Netfind by Telnet is not pretty to look at; you'll have to pay close attention to the screen. Further, these connections are sometimes busy, so you won't always get in; when you do, remember to allow for lagtime.

20.4 Gopher Searching

Consider Gopher as a library for browsing. From your campus server, you will usually find a directory that says, Other Gophers and Information Systems, or Online Libraries and Other Media. These are good starting places for browsing. We can't recommend browsing enough as an activity. For example, if you browse your way into an Other Gophers directory, you'll find an array of ways to go from there, including All the Gophers in the World. If you choose that option, you are taken down more and more narrow paths. You can go from the World, to North America, to the United States, to Vermont, to Johnson State College, a small, state school in one of the most breathtaking counties in the United States. You can travel anywhere, to any Gopher server's collection of information in the world you want.

You will also find subject-oriented Gopher directories. These break down Gopher directories by subject; PEG and Gopher Jewels are two of our favorites. By choosing literature as a subject, you can find thousands of online texts, critical studies, educational databases (such as ERIC digests), online literary journals, essays by other students, book reviews, and other useful data.

Your first online activity, after getting started in e-mail, should always be browsing. It's the best way to learn your way around; remember to use your bookmarks.

20.5 Veronica and WAIS

Veronica

You should practice using these search engines. We mentioned Veronica earlier as a way to look for a friend's school Gopher server. Veronica searches directory titles. This is fine for searches as specific as the name of a school; only so many directories will say University of Minnesota, for example, and chances are, if there are more than one, it won't matter too much to you because they all lead to the same place. However, if you are searching to find out as much information as you can on a topic, say, Shakespeare,

Veronica might be a little frustrating. It will find every directory that mentions Shakespeare. What you will find is that the directory titles will often be links to the same information. Furthermore, because you will have so many directories to search through for some searches (literature might get you around 400, for example), you should save the search results to your bookmark file. Once you get the list of results, which will be a list of links, type **a**, to save your current directory. Then you can return and work through longer results a little at a time.

Practice using Veronica by experimenting in the following:

The name of an author you are reading in class (you are less likely to have success with some contemporary authors)

The name of a setting of a book

Variations on themes from a book: Native American (perhaps if you are reading James Fenimore Cooper); whale (if you are reading Melville)

WAIS

WAIS, or Wide Area Information Search, does not search in as wide a geographical area as Veronica, but it does search multiple databases that have been connected to the WAIS search engine. Because its focus is narrower, you can do more complicated searches within the range. For example, it will search for key words, not just in the Gopher title or subject line of a directory, but also in the documents themselves. Using WAIS will be easier if you have a fuller sense of Boolean searching. In Boolean searching, you use the terms *AND*, *NOT*, or *OR* to define the scope of a search.

Search Command	Search Action Will Give
Edgar Allen Poe	Any source that has either Edgar, Allen, or Poe in it
Edgar AND Allen AND Poe	Any source that has *only* all three words in it
Edgar AND Allen OR Poe	Any source with only Edgar and Allen as a pair, or Poe alone (you can vary the search in many ways)

Edgar NOT Poe

Any source with Edgar, as 1ong as Poe is not also in the source

Educat*

Any source in which educat is part of a word (educate, education, educational, and so on)

It takes some practice getting used to Boolean searches. When a search returns results, they are referred to as "hits." Experiment with using the search; keep track of how many hits you get. Then look at the quality of the hits. More hits does not always mean you had a good search. If you wanted information about Edgar Allen Poe, the first search would result in more hits than the second. However, the second narrows the finds to those about the poet.

20.6 Searching the Web

You can apply searches to the WWW. Compare the finds you get in Gopher to those you get in the WWW. Compare search engines within the Web itself. Here are some search sites for you to explore:

WebCrawler   http://webcrawler.com/
Lycos   http://www.lycos.com/
Alta Vista   http://altavista.digital.com/
Jump City   http://www.jumpcity.com/
Info Seek   http://www.infoseek.com/
Excite   http://www.excite.com./
Deja News   http://www.dejanews.com/

Deja News searches USENET groups.

GLOSSARY

* The asterisk is used as a wildcard with commands to mean "all." For example, if in UNIX you wanted to remove a bunch of files that began with th, such as this.01, this.02, and this.03, you could enter **rm th*.0*** and all the files that begin with th would be removed. The asterisk frequently appears as shorthand as well. To refer to MOOs, MUDs, and MUSHs efficiently, people often write M*s.

Alias Sometimes people use this as a synonym for your login name. In that sense, it is short for the phrase ALso Identified AS. However, alias is also a UNIX command. You can create an alias for something you do often. For example, typing **alias daedalus Telnet MOO.daedalus.com 7777** at your prompt creates an alias called daedalus, which performs the same function as typing **telnet MOO.daedalus.com 7777**.

Archie Named after that famed Smallville teen, Archie allows users to search anonymous File Transfer Protocol (FTP) sites for files.

ARPANet Advanced Research Projects Administration Network. The system that laid the groundwork for the Internet. It was developed by the Department of Defense as a way to allow scientists working on defense projects to transfer data more rapidly. It was also intended as a network that could survive a nuclear war, a feat accomplished by assuring there was no central, controlling computer.

Article A synonym for an e-mail message posted to USENET, sometimes referred to simply as a post.

223

ASCII   American Standard Code for Information Interchange. This code is used for writing numbers, letters, and symbols without formatting particular to one word processing or editing program. A useful equivalent found on most word processors is the option to save a file as text only.

Bandwidth   The amount of data a line can move. As we move to fiber optics, we increase bandwidth—more data can be moved at faster speeds.

BBS   Bulletin Board System. An electronic meeting place organized by software that allows users to exchange mail, hold discussions, and swap files. Some BBSs offer Internet access, such as The Well, America Online, Prodigy, and CompuServe.

Binhex   BINary HEXadecimal. It converts nontext files into ASCII. This allows these files, often software, to be e-mailed. Binhex is a format associated with Macintosh, and many files found in Mac software archives are in binhex format with an .hqx file extension as part of their name. To use these files, they have to be "unbinhexed"—converted from ASCII to nontext format—after you download them to your Mac.

Bit   Binary digIT. The smallest part of computer data. Binary systems rely on a combination of 1s and 0s to create a bit. Bits combine to form bytes. Bits are also used as a way to measure bandwidth (how much information can be moved); a modem, for example, may operate at 9,600 bps, or bits per second.

BITNET   Because It's Time NETwork. BITNET is one of the original academic networks, but now much of BITNET has switched to the Internet's .edu domain. BITNET is still in place, and e-mail can move freely between BITNET and Internet.

Browser   A program that allows you to "see" and use Internet tools. For example, Mosaic is a World Wide Web browser that lets you navigate and see what's on the World Wide Web (see also *client*).

Byte   About 8 to 10 bits make a byte. Bytes combine to make other data, such as words.

Client   Software that reaches into the Internet and can bring things back for you. Gopher is a good example. In Gopher, links to other sights are already made for you and presented in a numbered menu. Gopher also contains components that allow you to download or mail what you find. Sometimes a client will bring you to files, and sometimes it will bring you to other software—ERIC, for example, or a BBS—which you must then log into.

CMC Computer Mediated Communication. This refers to tools used via a computer to communicate with others. CMC is generally broken into two broad categories, synchronous (real-time) and asynchronous. E-mail, BBS postings, USENET, file sharing are examples of asynchronous. That means the communication happens over time. A message posted to a discussion list is not likely to be read by everyone on the list the second you post it.

Real-time or synchronous CMC includes CUSEEME (real-time videoconferencing) software, MOOs, MUDs, IRC, and in some classrooms, products such as Daedalus's Interchange, Norton's Connect, or Houghton Mifflin's CommonSpace.

Cyberspace Coined by William Gibson in his novel *Neuromancer*, most people use the word to describe the Internet or other virtual environments (such as BBSs, LANs, and MOOs). The metaphor implies limitless, formless, and ultimately unknowable space that invites us to explore it. Compare that to a metaphor like the information superhighway, and you can begin to see how metaphors really go a long way in determining how we think about and, ultimately, use computers.

Domain Name System Sometimes referred to as DNS, it is a method for identifying an Internet host computer. The domain name uses words and abbreviations to correspond to router numbers assigned to the domain. The ending tells you about the type of site the domain is. Common endings are:

edu	for educational
gov	for government
com	for a business or person accessing from a commercial provider
ca	for Canada
Net	often for an Internet service provider
uk	for United Kingdom
org	usually for a nonprofit organization

Elm Electronic mail for UNIX. Elm is freeware, which means you can get a copy and use it at no cost.

Ethernet A networking method that allows computers to share data. Ethernet is used to describe a range of network wiring methods and speeds. In essence, Ethernet is like the switching station at a busy railroad terminal. It determines the speed and order of data movement.

FAQs Frequently Asked Questions. FAQs list and answer the most common questions on a particular subject. Usually the subject is a USENET group or discussion list, but it can also be about software or an Internet site.

Flame In computer mediated communication (CMC)—e-mail and chat programs—a flame, at its worst and most obvious, is an invective, acrimonious, ad hominen, intolerant, and scurrilous message. However, many times, mild disagreements are taken as flames when no flaming was intended. Often flames occur because a message meant as ironic or sarcastic is mistaken for intentional.

FTP File Transfer Protocol. A protocol, or method, for transferring a file from one computer to another via the Internet. FTP allows a user to login to another Internet site for retrieving a file there. Many Internet sites provide publicly accessible archives that anyone can access by using the login name "anonymous."

Gopher A menued system for accessing information on the Internet. Usually accessed by typing **gopher** at your account prompt, the software allows universities and other sites to link to other information and also to organize their own information for visitors and people on their campus.

Host A computer that is directly connected to the Internet. For most of you, it is the computer at your school on which you have your account. When you use your account, you are accessing the host and are allowed to run certain programs and services that are stored on the host, such as Gopher or an e-mail program.

HTML HyperText Markup Language. The coding language that creates hypertext documents for use on the World Wide Web. HTML works by inserting directions in and around text for web browsers to follow when they access a page.

HTTP HyperText Transport Protocol. The protocol for linking to files in hyptertext format. HTTP is the main protocol used in the World Wide Web (WWW).

Hypertext A system for organizing information in nodes and links. In hypertext, a node is a segment of information; on the World Wide Web, nodes are called pages. Within a page, a writer can create a link. The link can lead to another page; another Internet service or site such as Gopher or FTP; or a graphic image, audio clip, or video clip.

Internet The "too vast to accurately count" connection of computers and computer networks around the world. When you are on the Internet, you are on the network that evolved from the ARPANet project and are accessing via a machine that follows TCP/IP protocols.

internet Short for internetwork. Any two or more networks that are connected are internetworked, and thus form an internet. Some internets are connected to the Internet. There are many internets, but only one Internet.

IP Internet Protocol. The rules that determine how information travels on the Internet and how the collection of computers is networked. Often found in other acronyms such as SLIP or TCP/IP.

IP Number A particular number assigned to an Internet host. No two hosts share the same number. Since numbers are hard to remember, most numbers receive a corresponding domain name. However, more than one domain name can be linked to a number.

IRC Internet Relay Chat. A huge, largely ungoverned Internet-based chat system. It works by accessing IRC servers (and there are a number of them). The servers are linked to one another. Once linked, a user can create a channel or join already created channels. Then, any message a user writes and sends to the channel will be seen almost instantaneously by other users who are on the same channel. Likewise, the user will see any messages other users send. In this way, users can swap messages or chat. The servers relay the messages. IRC is an example of synchronous or real-time computer mediated communication (CMC).

Kilobyte A thousand bytes. Actually it's 1024 bytes, but everyone rounds it off. Often written as just K, as in "I downloaded a 19K file" (see also *byte, bit*).

LAN Local Area Network. A computer network with a short reach, usually the networking of computers in one area such as a building or classroom. If a LAN becomes linked to a larger network, such as the Internet, it is sometimes referred to as a WAN, or wide area network. However, it might help to think in more geographic terms: LAN, one room or building; WAN, one location or company, as on a college campus; and Internet, beyond one room, certainly, but also beyond one institution's domain.

Listproc Software for managing e-mail distribution lists.

Listserv Popular e-mail list distribution software. Listserv originated on BITNET lists, and if you access USENET, you'll see many groups in the bit.listserv.* hierarchy. This reflects that origin; however, not all those groups (bit.listserv.mbu-1, for example) are BITNET based. In fact, MBU is now Internet based and uses listproc software.

Login As a verb, it means the process of logging into a system: "I find the Internet fascinating, so I login everyday." As an adjective, it usually describes some part of the login procedure: "What is your login name?" As a noun it usually refers to the place in a program or protocol where you do the logging in: "Go to the login and enter your username."

Megabyte A million bytes. A thousand kilobytes. Often written as just MB, as in "I installed a 2MB software program" (see also *byte, bit, kilobyte*).

Modem MOdulator, DEModulator. A device that allows your computer to use a phone line so that your computer can access other computers.

MOO MUD, Object Oriented. The key here is object oriented. A MOO, like a MUD, is primarily a text-based, multiple-user program. Object oriented refers to object-oriented programming, which allows programmers to integrate pieces of programming from other programs into their own designs.

Mosaic A graphic web browser.

MUD Multi-User Dungeon, or Dimension. "Dimension" is a more recent, more system-manager-friendly term. "Dungeon" is the original term because the first MUDs were used to play Dungeons and Dragons.

Multimedia Documents, programs, and products (CD-ROM encyclopedias, for example) that include different kinds of media—text, graphics, audio, and moving images—to convey information. When the information is more integrated and tied to a hypertext system, the term *hypermedia* might be used.

Netscape The successor to Mosaic as the most popular program for accessing the WWW.

Network Two or more computers that are connected and can share resources constitute a network.

Newsgroups The names for discussion groups on USENET.

NIC   Network Information Center. Any office that manages network information. In colleges, similar duties might be assigned to OIT (Office of Instructional Technologies) or UCS (University Computing Services). That is, not every site uses the term. The most famous, and perhaps most important, NIC is InterNIC, which registers new domain names for computers as they come onto the Internet.

NNTP   Network News Transfer Protocol. Not something you'll ever have to worry about, but you might see it referred to. It's the method used to send USENET messages.

Node   Any single computer on a network. In some hypertext lexicons, nodes refer to units of information.

Packet   A collection of data. Information is broken into packets, usually about 1500 bytes long, which traverse the Internet independently. Each packet has the address of where it came from and where it's going. Packets share data lines with other packets, much the way commuters share a subway ride. As packets arrive at their destination, they regroup to form the entire set of information.

Password   What you need to know to log into some systems. A good password is your best protection against someone using your account. Good passwords use a combination of letters and nonletters. They should not be too simple, like Sick1, and should avoid using numbers significant to a user, such as a birth date or license plate number. A random combination of letters, numbers, and symbols (where allowed) works best, such as H7&B3-Q.

PINE   Program for Internet News and E-mail. A very popular program for sending e-mail and reading USENET News. It was designed for beginners, but can be set for more advanced uses by experienced users. PINE is also sometimes referred to (though not officially) as Pine Is Not Elm to distinguish it from Elm, an earlier and still popular e-mail program.

Port   This has two meanings. One refers to the physical input/output sockets you see on the back of your computer: one might be for a modem, one for a keyboard, one for a printer. Another use of port is to identify a particular Internet application. For example, many MOO addresses contain a port number. You'll usually see it in the instructions: Telnet some.MOO.com 7777. In this example, the 7777 represents the port number.

Post An individual article sent to a USENET newsgroup. People sometimes carry this term over and use it for messages sent to e-mail discussion lists (also known as posting).

PPP Point to Point Protocol. Allows a computer to use a regular telephone line and a modem to make a TCP/IP connection and thus be really and truly on the Internet. PPP is gradually replacing SLIP for this purpose. Many people use a PPP connection with a high-speed modem to take full advantage of the World Wide Web.

RTFM Read the [fine old Anglo-Saxon word] Manual. A common abbreviation in computerdom, usually used by one annoyed by too many questions.

Server Software that allows a computer to run programs or make information available to other computers. The term refers to the software or the machine on which the server software is stored.

Signature A file, usually about five to six lines long, appended to the end of e-mail or USENET messages. The file will contain a sender's name and e-mail address at a minimum, but just as often includes snail mail addresses, quotes, disclaimers, and every once in a while, a copyright claim (also known as sig. or sig. file).

SLIP Serial Line Internet Protocol. A method for using a telephone line and modem to connect a computer to the Internet directly and use the Internet fully. SLIP is gradually being replaced by PPP.

Smiley Smilies, or smiley faces, sometimes called emoticons, provide a visual clue to a writer's intent. Common examples include :-) for happy, :-(for sad, and ;-) for just kidding or humor intended.

TCP/IP Transmission Control Protocol/Internet Protocol. These combined protocols define the Internet. To really be on the Internet, your computer must have TCP/IP software. Don't fret; this is becoming easier to do as modems become faster; the most recent generation of computers usually include this software in the bundling.

Telnet A method for connecting to a remote computer and using software or accessing information on that computer.

Terminal A terminal lets you send commands to a computer that is somewhere else. Usually, your keyboard and display screen or monitor will use software that allows it to emulate a terminal (called, naturally enough, terminal emulation software).

Timeout What will happen when one computer fails to answer another. If, for example, you Telnet to another computer, there may be a wait for the connection to go through. However, if the connection is not made in a set amount of time, you will be timed out and will find yourself back at the prompt from which you launched the Telnet command.

tn3270 A version of Telnet that interacts properly with IBM mainframes.

UNIX The most common operating system for servers on the Internet, UNIX has TCP/IP built into it and was designed for multiusers. You do not have to use UNIX to use the Internet, but chances are you will run into it in your travels.

URL Uniform Resource Locator. The method for writing addresses to any resource that can be accessed via the WWW. The beginning of the URL will indicate the resource type: http = hypertext, gopher = gopher, mailto = allows e-mailing, news = connects to Usenet, telnet = allows user to telnet, ftp = connects to FTP server.

Sample URLs:

http://www.umass.edu/english/nickhome.html

mailto:nickc@english.umass.edu

news:new.newusers.questions

gopher://ericir.syr.edu:70/11/Clearinghouses/16houses/CLL

USENET A collection of discussion groups that exchange messages. USENET is worldwide, decentralized, sometimes anarchic, diverse, and accessible on the Internet though it does predate the Internet. Last time we checked, more than 10,000 newsgroups were on USENET. Your site may not subscribe to them all.

Veronica Very Easy Rodent Oriented Net-wide Index to Computerized Archives. A tool on Gopher for searching Gopher menus by word. It will find directories and files that contain the word you search for.

WAIS Wide Area Information Search Software that allows the indexing (and searching of those indexes) of information. WAIS ranks search results by relevance to request; subsequent searches can be based on prior searches, allowing a searcher to hone his or her queries.

WAN   Wide Area Network. Any network that extends beyond a single building or campus.

WWW   World Wide Web. A hypertext-based system for navigating the Internet and using all its tools: Gopher, FTP, http, Telnet, tn3270, USENET, e-mail, WAIS, MUDs and MOOs, and so on. World Wide Web also refers to the various servers that allow text, video, audio, and graphic files to be combined in hypertext.

INDEX

Acceptable use policy (AUP), 8–9, 11, 121
Acknowledgment message, 44
Acronyms, list, 26
Activities for students, 214–221
  e-mail address searches, 217–219
  Gopher searches, 219
  USENET for English classes, 214–216
  USENET for yourself, 213-214
  Veronica searches, 219–220
  WAIS searches, 220–221
  WWW searches, 221
ACW (Alliance for Computers and Writing), 67–68, 159, 197–198
Address book, e-mail, 31–33, 217
Addresses
  alias file or book, 31–33, 217
  in e-mail, 12, 27–28, 30, 196–197, 217–219
  in Gopher, 65, 68–70
  in Lynx, 65, 70–71
  in MOOs and MUDs, 112
  in WWW, 69
  URLs, 69, 99–100
Advanced Research Projects Agency, Defense Department (ARPA), 5
Aladdin Systems homepage, 87–88
Aleks, Norman, 39
Alias file, e-mail, 31–33, 217
Alliance for Computers and Writing (ACW), 67–68, 159, 197–198
American Psychological Association (APA). See APA style guidelines
America Online (AOL), 88, 174–175, 221
Andreeson, Marc, 103
Angle brackets (< >), 131, 132
Anonymous FTP, 77–83, 90–95; see also FTP
AOL (America Online), 88, 174–175, 221
APA (American Psychological Association) style guidelines, 167–171
  e-mail citations, 169–170

FTP citations, 171
Gopher citations, 171
MOO or MUD citations, 170–171
standard elements, 167–168
WWW citations, 171
Apple Macintosh. *See* Macintosh, Apple
Applets, 97
Archie, 74, 194
Archives, electronic text, 152, 204
Archives, mailing list, 48–51
database search of, 49–51
index files, 48–49, 51, 52
retrieving, 49, 51, 52
via Web and Gopher, 52–53
Archives, public file. *See* Public file archives
ARPA (Advanced Research Projects Agency, Defense Department), 5
ASCII (text) files, 33, 64, 73
AUP (acceptable use policy), 8–9, 11, 121
Auto image load, 100–101
Automatic login, 59

Because It's Time Network (BITNET), 38
Binary files, 73, 93–95
BinHex extension, 95, 137
BITNET (Because It's Time Network), 38
Bookmarking, 65–68, 74, 75
in Gopher, 65–67
in Lynx, 67–68
in Mosaic (hotlists), 104
in Netscape, 99
Books about the Internet, 206–207
Boolean searching, 218, 220
Boyer, Calvin, 195

Carnegie Mellon University's English Server, 149, 202
Case sensitivity
of Gopher, 19, 74
of Lynx, 75
of UNIX, 18–19, 59, 78, 137
Chapman, Brent, 38
Chicago Manual of Style (CMS)
style guidelines, 172–183
bibliographic format, 173
database citations, 173–174
e-mail citations, 174–179
FTP citations, 181–182
Gopher citations, 182
information service citations, 173–174
in-text format, 173
MOO or MUD citations, 179–181
WWW citations, 183
Citation of sources, 9, 15, 154–183
APA style, 167–171
Chicago (CMS) style, 172–183
guidelines, 158–183
MLA style, 159–167
pagination problems, 156-157
tips on correct, 154–155
version numbers, 156
working with Internet files, 155–158
see also Copyright issues
Clients, MOO and MUD, 112–114
CMS (*Chicago Manual of Style*). *See Chicago Manual of Style* (CMS) style guidelines
Commands
e-mail, 40–43, 45–48
FTP, 78–79
Gopher, 74–75
Lynx, 75-76

MOOs and MUDs, 118
Telnetting, 58–62
UNIX, 129–131, 137–139
Compression, file, 80–83,
    87–89, 112–114
Compuserve, 174–175
Copyright issues, 143–153
    brand name sources,
        148–149
    complexities of collaboration,
        147
    copyright violation hazards,
        145–146
    honesty, 146–148
    introduction, 144
    new forms of scholarship,
        145–146, 151
    paper vs. pixels, 144–145
    peer reviewed sources,
        150–151
    plagiarism, 144–146
    quoting, 152–153
    stability of sources, 145–146
    standards, 144, 147, 150
    see also Citation of sources
Corio, Ron, 167, 169
Corporation for Research and
    Educational Networking
    (CREN), 38
Creating a web page. See Web
    pages
CREN (Corporation for Research
    and Educational
    Networking), 38
Cross-posting, 122
Crump, Eric, 189
Cybermind homepage, 53
Cybertutors, 124–125

DaedalusMOO, 116–117, 120
Databases, telnetting to, 58–62
DEC (Digital Equipment
    Corporation), 92–93, 194

Decompression software,
    82–83, 87–89, 112–114
Default page, in graphic
    browsers, 100, 104
Digital Equipment Corporation
    (DEC), 92–93, 194
Directories of Internet
    resources, 188–189
Directory of Scholarly
    Electronic Conferences,
        188–189
Disinfectant, 85
Disney's Toy Story homepage,
    64–65
DNS (Domain Name System),
    27–28
Domain names, 27–28
Downloading files
    with e-mail, 33–34
    with FTP, 77–83, 90–95
    with Gopher, 73–74
    with Lynx, 73–74
    protocols for, 73–74
    from public archives, 86,
        90–95

Educational Resources
    Information Center
    (ERIC), 59, 167, 173,
        200
E-mail, 25–35
    acronyms in, 26
    address book use, 31–33, 217
    addresses, 12, 27–28, 30,
        196–197, 217–219
    basics of, 25–35
    citing as source, 160–162,
        169–170, 174–181
    emoticons in, 26–27, 209
    ending a message, 30–31
    file transfer by, 33–34
    flames, 9–10, 14, 34–35
    in graphic browsers, 101, 104

introduction, 23–24
lingo of, 25–27
netiquette for, 9, 11–14, 209
replying, 29–30
saving messages, 33
signing, 12, 30–31
spams, 34
subject line, 12, 25, 28-29
see also Mailing lists
Emoticons, 26–27, 209
English Online homepage, 7, 20
English-specific resources. *See* Resources for English majors
English students, relevance of Internet to, 5–7
ERIC (Educational Resources Information Center), 59, 166, 173, 200
Eudora, 31
eWorld, 88
Expectations for this book, 7

Failed connection messages, 92
Files
ASCII (text), 33, 64, 73
binary, 73
citing Internet, 154–183
compressed, 80–83, 87–89
decompressing, 82–83, 87–89, 112–114
downloading, 73–74, 77–83, 90–95
links to in web pages, 134–135
MacBinary, 73
public archives, 90–95
saving, 71–72
user permissions, 130–131
File Transfer Protocol. *See* FTP
Flames, 9–10, 14, 34–35
Freeware, 85, 90–95

FTP (File Transfer Protocol), 64, 77–83
anonymous, 78–83
citing as source, 162–163, 171, 181–182
commands, 78–79
by e-mail, 33–34
introduction, 77–78
navigating directories, 79–81
public archives and, 90–95
search engines for, 74
sites, 89–90

Game playing, 108–109
Goldpaugh, Tom, 197
Gopher, 63–76
addresses, 68–70
bookmarking, 65–67
case sensitivity of, 19, 74
citing as source, 163–164, 171, 182–183
commands, 74–75
downloading files, 73–74
introduction, 63–65
mailing list archives and, 52
navigating, 65, 68–70
public file archives and, 86
saving a file in, 71–72
searching, 74, 195–196, 219
Gopher Jewels, 195–196, 219
Gopherspace, 63, 68
Government resources, 204–205
Graphic browsers, 64–65, 96–107
default page in, 100, 104
helper applications, 97
introduction, 96–97
Java language, 97
MacWeb, 105–107
Mosaic, 102–105, 209
Netscape, 97–102, 209
sites, 102, 105, 107, 209–210

URLs to explore, 102, 105, 107
WinWeb, 105–107
Graphic interface, 96–97
Gutenberg Project, 152, 204

Harris, Steven R., 196, 199,
    208
Harvard's Online Library
    Information Service
    (HOLLIS), 59–62,
    166–167, 173–174
Headers, e-mail, 29
Headings, HTML, 133
Helper applications, 97
Help with the Internet, 191,
    206–210
  e-mail guides, 209
  netiquette guides, 209
  online books, 206–207
  online guides, 192, 207
  printed books, 207
  sites for tools, 102, 105,
    107, 209–210
  WWW help, 208–209
HOLLIS (Harvard's Online
    Library Information
    Service), 59–62,
    166–167, 173–174
Homepages. See Web pages
Hot Java, 97
Hotlists (bookmarks), Mosaic,
    104
Houghton Mifflin Company
    homepage, 7, 149
HREF links, HTML, 134
HTML (Hypertext Markup
    Language)
  basics, 132–135
  editors, 129
  graphic browsers and, 98–99
  headings, 133
  image sources, 134–135
  introduction, 131–132

learning, 129–130, 208
lists, 133
links, 134–135
paragraphs, 133
sample document, 135–137
tags, 131–135
USENET group on, 191
viewing web page source,
    101–102, 104
Hypermail, 53
Hypertext, 131–132
Hypertext Markup Language
    (HTML). See HTML
Hypertext Reference tags, 134

Image map, 65
Images, in web pages, 134–135
Image sources, HTML, 134–135
Indexes, mailing list, 39–40
INFO-Mac, 89–90, 93–94
Interest groups, mailing list, 40
Interfaces with the Net, 16–17,
    96–97
International Standards
    Organization (ISO), 172
Internet
  activities for students,
    214–221
  citation of sources, 154–183
  copyright issues, 143–153
  creating a WWW page,
    128–139
  defined, 3–4
  electronic mail, 25–35
  file transfer protocol (FTP),
    64, 77–83
  Gopher, 63–76
  graphic browsers, 64–65,
    96–107
  help, 191, 206–210
  history, 4–5
  introduction, 1–7
  Lynx, 63–76

mailing lists, 36–57
MOOS, 108–122
MUDS, 108–122
netiquette, 8–15, 121–122
OWLS, 123–127
preparing to enter, 16–20
public file archives, 84–95
relevance to English students,
    5–7
resources for English students,
    187–205
Telnetting, 58–62, 109–112
text-based tools, 58–76
WIOLEs, 125–127
Internet Relay Chat (IRC), 126
ISO (International Standards
    Organization), 172

Java, 97, 210
Journals, online, 150–151,
    202–204

Kehoe, Brendan, 162–163
Kemp, Fred, 155
Kotsikonas, Anastasios, 38
Kovacs, Diane, 188

Lag time, 62
Learning online resources.
    See Resources for
    English majors
Lee, Abraham, 167, 169
Links, HTML, 134–135
Links, WWW, 65–66
    bookmarking, 65–68, 74–75,
        99, 104
    defined, 65
    navigating, 65, 68–71
Listproc
    archives and, 51
    described, 38–39
    getting help, 56
    mail options, 47–48

subscribing in, 42–43
unsubscribing in, 44
viewing current mail settings,
    47–48
Listprocessor. *See* Listproc
Lists, HTML, 133
Lists, mailing. *See* Mailing lists
Listserv
    archives and, 48–51
    command protocol, 41
    described, 38–39
    getting help, 55–56
    list indexes, 39–40
    mail options, 45–47
    subscribing in, 41–42
    unsubscribing in, 43–44
    viewing current mail settings,
        46
Lists of lists, 39–40
Literature resources. *See*
    Resources for English
    majors
Log files, 49
Login
    automatic, 59
    in FTP, 78–79
L-Soft International, 38
Lycos, 194, 217–218, 221
Lynx, 63–76
    addresses, 65, 70–71
    bookmarking, 65–66, 67–68
    commands, 75–76
    downloading files, 73–74
    introduction, 63–65
    lowercase sensitivity, 75
    navigating in, 65, 70–71
    saving a file in, 72
    searching, 74

Macintosh, Apple
    decompression utilities,
        87–89
    graphic web browsers,
        96–107
    MacBinary files, 73

software archives, 89–90
MacWeb, 105–107
Magazines, online, 203–204
Mailing lists, 36–57
    archives, 48–53
    common problems, 53–55
    finding, 39–40
    help, 55–57
    how they work, 37–38
    indexes, 39–40
    introduction, 36–37
    lists of lists, 39–40
    log files, 49
    mail options, 45–48
    software for, 38–39
    subscribing, 40–43
    unsubscribing, 43–45
    for writing and literature,
        189–190
Mailing list software, 38–39;
        see also Listproc;
        Listserv; Majordomo
Mail options, 45–48
Majordomo
    archives and, 52
    described, 38–39
    getting help, 56, 191
    mail options, 48
    subscribing in, 43
    unsubscribing in, 44–45
Makulovich, John, 196
Mallon, Thomas, 146
MediaMOO, 117
MEDLIT, 173
Megabyte University, 42–43,
        155, 161, 190
Merit Software Archives, 86,
        210
Message of the day (MOD), 91
Messages, e-mail
    addresses, 12, 27–28, 30
    composing, 12–14
    cross-posting, 12
    flames, 34–35
    netiquette, 11–14
    replying to, 29–30

saving, 33
signatures, 30–31
spams, 34
subject lines, 12, 25, 28–29
see also E-mail; Mailing lists
Metacrawler, 195
Microsoft Windows. See
        Windows, Microsoft
Mirror sites, 89–90
MLA (Modern Language
        Association) style
        guidelines, 159–167
    e-mail citations, 160–162
    FTP citations, 162–163
    Gopher citations, 163–164
    MOO or MUD citations,
        162, 165–166
    Telnet citations, 166–167
    text citations, 166–167
    works-cited entry, 159–160
    WWW citations, 164
MOD (message of the day), 91
Modern Language Association
        (MLA). See MLA style
        guidelines
Mogensen, Christian, 208
MOOs (MUDs, Object-
        Oriented), 108–122
    addresses, 112
    citing as source, 162, 165–166,
        170–171, 178–181
    clients, 110, 112–114
    commands, 118
    etiquette, 121–122
    help, 109, 118–119, 201
    introduction, 108–109
    Munchkin example character,
        115–116
    objects in, 179–180
    page scrolling, 110–111, 117
    participants' names, 162,
        170, 178
    sample session, 115–122
    sending a message, 111–112
    sites, 201
    Telnetting, 109–112

wordwrap, 110, 117
Mosaic, 103–105
    default page, 104
    e-mail, 104
    hotlist feature, 104
    introduction, 102–104
    Netnews (USENET) reader,
        104
    view source feature, 104
    where to find, 105
MUDDweller, 110
MUDs, Object-Oriented
        (MOOs). *See* MOOs
MUDs (Multi-User
Dimensions),
        108–114; *see also* MOOs
Munchkin, 115–116

National Center for
        Supercomputer
        Applications (NCSA),
        96, 103, 104, 105
Navigating
    directories, 79–81
    in Gopher, 65, 68–70
    links, 65–71
    in Lynx, 65, 70–71
NCSA (National Center for
        Supercomputer
        Applications), 96, 103,
        104, 105
NetFind, 218–219
Netiquette, 8–15
    acceptable use policies,
        9–11, 121
    access rules, 9, 11
    decorum rules, 9, 14
    defined, 8, 10
    e-mail rules, 9, 14
    flames, 14
    help, 209
    in MOOs and MUDs,
        121–122
    privacy, 10

quick reference, 9
research citation rules, 9, 15,
        159–183
Netnews (USENET) readers,
        101, 104
Netscape, 97–102
    bookmark feature, 99
    default page, 100
    e-mail, 101
    frames, 98–99
    history feature, 99
    interface elements, 100–101
    introduction, 97–99
    location feature, 99–100
    Netnews (USENET) reader,
        101
    viewing HTML source,
        101–102
    where to find, 102
Netscape Communications
        Corporation, 98, 100,
        102
Newbie Net, 191, 207
Norstad, John, 85

Online Computer Library
        Center, 150
Online journals, 150–151,
        202–204
Online Writery, 120, 124,
        125–126, 135–136
OWLs (Online Writing Labs),
        123–125, 126–127,
        199–200

PageMill, 129
Paragraphs, HTML, 133
Passwords, 10
Permissions, file, 130–131
Plagiarism
    college standards, 144
    honesty, 145, 146–148
    introduction, 144

quoting, 152–153
  see also Citation of sources;
    Copyright issues
Point to Point Protocol (PPP),
  73, 78
Postal mail, 24, 25
PPP (Point to Point Protocol),
  73, 78
Preparing for the Internet,
  16–20
  enormousness of the Net,
    19–20
  learning and error, 17–19
  software for, 17, 18–19
  varied interfaces, 16–17
Prodigy, 174–175
Project Gutenberg, 152, 204
Prompt line, 60
Publications online, 201–204
Public file archives, 84–95
  decompression utilities and,
    87–89
  downloading files, 86,
    90–95
  freeware, 85, 90–95
  FTP from, 90–95
  introduction, 84–85
  shareware, 85, 90–95
  sites, 89–90

Quoting, e-mail, 9, 14

Research, online
  citation of sources, 154–183
  copyright issues, 143–153
  keeping a log, 147
  resources, 187–205
  search tools, 194–197,
    214–221
  Telnetting to databases,
    58–62
  writing portfolio, 147
  see also Citation of sources;

Resources for English majors;
  Search tools, online
Resources for English majors,
  187–205
  directories of, 187–188
  e-mail lists, 189–190
  English-specific, 197–198
  general education, 200
  government, 204–205
  literature and the humanities,
    198–199
  MOO and MUD, 201
  online projects, 204
  online writing labs, 199–200
  publications, 201–204
  search tools, 192–197
  USENET groups, 190–192
Revised List Processor. *See*
  Listserv
RhetNet, 132, 202

Screen capture, as help tool, 114
Search tools, online, 194–197,
    214–221
  Archie, 74, 194
  Digital's program, 194
  direct (keyword) searches,
    194–195
  finding e-mail addresses,
    196–197, 217–219
  for Gopher, 74, 195–196, 219
  Lycos, 194, 217–218, 221
  Metacrawler, 195
  NetFind, 218–219
  phone and address books,
    196–197
  subject-categorized searches,
    195–197
  undirected searches, 195
  Veronica, 74, 194, 217,
    219–220
  for WAIS, 194, 220–221
  WebCrawler, 195, 217–218,
    221

for WWW, 194–195, 221
WWW Worm, 195, 221
Yahoo, 107–108, 196, 207
Security, e-mail, 10
Self-extracting archives, 87
Serial Line In Put (SLIP), 73, 78
Shareware, 85, 90–95
Shouting, 9
Signature files, 30–31
Sill, David, 163
Sites
    FTP, 89–90
    to get graphic browsers,
        102, 105, 107, 209–210
    mirror, 89–90
    OWL, 126–127
    public archive, 89–90
    URLs to explore, 107
    WIOLE, 126–127
    see also Public file archives
Slade, Robert, 172–173
Slash (/), 67, 132, 163, 176
SLIP (Serial Line In Put), 73, 78
Smileys, 26–27, 209
Software
    archives of, 84–95
    file compression, 82–83,
        87–89, 112–114
    graphic browsers, 96–107,
        209–210
    for Internet access, 17, 18–19
    mailing list, 38–39
    MOO and MUD clients,
        112–114
Software archives, public. See
    Public file archives
Sokolik, Maggi, 167, 169
"Snail mail," 24, 25
Spams, 34
Sparkle, 97
Student activities. See Activities
    for students
StuffIt Expander, 87–88, 137
Subject-categorized search
    tools, 195–197; see also
    Search tools, online

Subject line, e-mail, 12, 25,
    28–29, 41
Subscribing to mailing lists,
    40–43
Sun Microsystems, 97

Tags, HTML, 131–135
TCP/IP (Transmission Control
    Protocol/Internet
    Protocol), 5
Teaching English as a Second
    Language Electronic
    Journal, 167, 169, 203
Telnetting, 58–62, 64
    citing as source, 166–167,
        173
    connecting to a database,
        59–62
    introduction, 58–59
    lag time in, 62
    in MOOs, 109–112
Text (ASCII) files, 33, 64, 73
Text-based browsers, 58–76;
    see also Gopher; Lynx;
    Telnetting
Thomas, Eric, 38
Time Warner's Pathfinder Web
    News Service, 148–149,
    204
TinyFugue, 110, 112–114
TradeWave, 105, 107, 210
Transferring files. See
    Downloading files; FTP
Transmission Control Protocol/
    Internet Protocol
    (TCP/IP), 5
Turabian, Kate L., 172

Uniform Resource Locators.
    See URLs
UNIX operating system
    case sensitivity of, 18–19,
        59, 78, 137
    commands, 129–131, 137–139

decompressing files in,
112–114
downloading from, 92–93, 137
long filenames in, 95
web servers on, 129–130
Unsubscribing from mailing
lists, 43–45
Unzipping files, 82–83
Uploading files, by e-mail,
33–34
URLs (Uniform Resource
Locators)
of current location, 99–100
defined, 69, 71, 72
finding Mosaic, 105
finding Netscape, 102
in HTML links, 134
sites to explore, 107
USENET (global discussion list
service)
groups for writing and literature, 190–191
netiquette for, 8–15
news readers, 101, 104

Veronica, 74, 194, 217, 219–220
Video clips, 97
Viewing source, of web pages,
101–102, 104, 135
Virtual Machine/Conversational
Monitor System
(VM/CMS), 92–93, 95
Virus detection software, 85
VM/CMS (Virtual Machine/
Conversational Monitor
System), 92–93, 95
VMS (Digital Equipment
Corporation's operating
system), 92–93

WAIS, 194, 220–221
Walker, Janice R., 159, 164
Web. *See* World Wide Web
(WWW)

Web browsers. *See* Graphic
browsers; Text-based
browsers
WebCrawler, 195, 217–218,
221
Webliography, 196, 199
Web pages
creating, 128–139
default, 100, 104
HTML basics, 132–135
images in, 134–135
introduction, 128–129,
131–132
links to other places, 133
permissions for users,
130–131
UNIX commands, 129–131,
137–139
viewing HTML source,
101–102, 104
see also HTML
Windows, Microsoft
decompression utilities,
88–89
graphic web browsers,
96–107
software archives, 90
WinWeb, 105–107
WIOLEs (Writing Intensive
Online Learning
Environments), 125–127
World Wide Web (WWW)
citing as source, 164, 171,
183
creating your own page,
128–139
graphic browsers, 64–65,
96–107
help, 208–209
homepage for this book, 7
HTML coding, 98–99,
101–102, 104, 132–135
Lynx and, 63–76
searching, 194–195, 217–219,
221
text-based browsers, 58–76

World Wide Web Consortium
        homepage, 107, 208
Writing Across the Curriculum,
        190, 198
Writing Intensive Online
        Learning Environments
        (WIOLEs), 125–127
Writing resources. *See* Resources
        for English majors
WWW (World Wide Web). *See*
        World Wide Web
WWW Worm, 195, 221

Yahoo's World Wide Web
        Directory, 107–108,
        196, 207

Zip compression software,
        82–83, 88

E-Mail and Internet Address Book

Name _____   Name _____
Address _____   Address _____
_____   _____

Name _____   Name _____
Address _____   Address _____
_____   _____

Name _____   Name _____
Address _____   Address _____
_____   _____

Name _____   Name _____
Address _____   Address _____
_____   _____

Name _____   Name _____
Address _____   Address _____
_____   _____

Name _____   Name _____
Address _____   Address _____
_____   _____

Name _____   Name _____
Address _____   Address _____
_____   _____

Name _____   Name _____
Address _____   Address _____
_____   _____

Name _____   Name _____
Address _____   Address _____
_____   _____

Name _____   Name _____
Address _____   Address _____
_____   _____

Name _____	Name _____
Address _____	Address _____
_____	_____
Name _____	Name _____
Address _____	Address _____
_____	_____
Name _____	Name _____
Address _____	Address _____
_____	_____
Name _____	Name _____
Address _____	Address _____
_____	_____
Name _____	Name _____
Address _____	Address _____
_____	_____
Name _____	Name _____
Address _____	Address _____
_____	_____
Name _____	Name _____
Address _____	Address _____
_____	_____
Name _____	Name _____
Address _____	Address _____
_____	_____
Name _____	Name _____
Address _____	Address _____
_____	_____
Name _____	Name _____
Address _____	Address _____
_____	_____
Name _____	Name _____
Address _____	Address _____
_____	_____

Name _____	Name _____
Address _____	Address _____
_____	_____
Name _____	Name _____
Address _____	Address _____
_____	_____
Name _____	Name _____
Address _____	Address _____
_____	_____
Name _____	Name _____
Address _____	Address _____
_____	_____
Name _____	Name _____
Address _____	Address _____
_____	_____
Name _____	Name _____
Address _____	Address _____
_____	_____
Name _____	Name _____
Address _____	Address _____
_____	_____
Name _____	Name _____
Address _____	Address _____
_____	_____
Name _____	Name _____
Address _____	Address _____
_____	_____
Name _____	Name _____
Address _____	Address _____
_____	_____
Name _____	Name _____
Address _____	Address _____

Name _____   Name _____
Address _____   Address _____
_____   _____

Name _____   Name _____
Address _____   Address _____
_____   _____

Name _____   Name _____
Address _____   Address _____
_____   _____

Name _____   Name _____
Address _____   Address _____
_____   _____

Name _____   Name _____
Address _____   Address _____
_____   _____

Name _____   Name _____
Address _____   Address _____
_____   _____

Name _____   Name _____
Address _____   Address _____
_____   _____

Name _____   Name _____
Address _____   Address _____
_____   _____

Name _____   Name _____
Address _____   Address _____
_____   _____

Name _____   Name _____
Address _____   Address _____
_____   _____

Name _____   Name _____
Address _____   Address _____
_____   _____

Ms. Letbetter
Dr. Moore